Praise for *Find Your Voice*

"You've been waiting for what seems a lifetime to be heard and finally the world is ready. *Find Your Voice* is your go-to guidebook to help amplify your voice and connect your message to that which matters most to you. Tabby provides a beautiful blend of storytelling along with tools, resources and leadership practices that will take you off the sidelines, beyond your fears and into action."

— Elisa Parker, co-founder, President, See Jane Do

"Tabby Biddle has crafted a 21st century roadmap to owning your truth and harnessing it to positively change the world. Filled with personal accounts, practical action steps, and thought-provoking questions, *Find Your Voice* creates the possibility for women of all stages and ages in life to step into their innate greatness."

— Judith Martinez, founder and CEO, InHerShoes

"*Find Your Voice* will help you focus your goals and unleash your inner power to go after your passions and never look back. This book is must-read for any woman searching for more meaning in her life."

— Sarah Moshman, Emmy Award winning filmmaker and director, *The Empowerment Project*

"Tabby Biddle has a voice that incites us all to use our own. If you feel reticent, or even afraid to use your voice, *Find Your Voice* book is a sacred guide to give you the practical support to rise."

— Meggan Watterson, author of *Reveal*

"Tabby's commitment to women's and girls' empowerment is sincere and brave and it will inspire you to claim your power, own your message, take smart action, and use your brilliant voice – for you, for all of us!"

— **Paige Nolan,** writer, speaker and coach

"*Find Your Voice* is a bible for a woman in search of discovering her voice. This guide can help women go from just thinking about having a voice, to actually discovering it, and being motivated to share it. This book is all heart and chock full of anecdotes, personal stories and wonderful exercises that I simply couldn't put it down."

— **Giselle Shapiro,** founder of LiteraryLaunch.com

"This is a must-read book for all women. *Find Your Voice* is written with such a strong voice and equally powerful call to action that it's impossible to read it and not start writing your own blog and signature talk before having finished the book. I did just that."

— **Lotta Alsén,** international business consultant and founder of Quickenings

"After reading Tabby Biddle's *Find Your Voice*, I find myself looking at my life very differently. Traversing my own path toward self-expression feels less elusive, and my need to get there more critical. *Find Your Voice* takes you on a powerful journey and spits you out on the other side with a new-found sense of purpose, and an arsenal of tactics to find your voice and 'get out there' with it."

— **Lili Weigert,** writer and brand strategist

"*Find Your Voice* is an inspiring call to action for every woman who is holding back from communicating her truth with the world. As you read the book, you feel like Tabby is right there with you, encouraging you on your journey of self-discovery."

– Dakota Smith, elementary school teacher

"*Find Your Voice* is a must read for any woman who has ever been silenced. The energy of Tabby's determination to help us find our voice fills each page. As a woman who discovered her voice late in life, I appreciate what Tabby offers in the book to bring me back into my body and into my core. It feels safe and satisfying to not only have techniques that allow a smooth flow of power to be expressed, but to also know that I am not alone."

– Jen Duchene, author of *Le Chic Cocoon*

"*Find Your Voice* is the perfect book for any woman that feels like she has something more to say and do in the world. Tabby identifies the ingrained predisposition women have towards feeling unable to speak their truth and discusses how we can overcome our fear of using our voice to affect change. Filled with inspirational stories, thought-provoking questions, and a great resource list, I highly recommend this book. I am going to give it as a gift to all my girlfriends!"

– Mary Collier, author of *A Woman's Quest for Clarity*

FIND
YOUR VOICE

FIND
YOUR VOICE

A Woman's Call to Action

Tabby Biddle

Women Press

Los Angeles

Find Your Voice: A Woman's Call to Action

Copyright © 2015 by Tabby Biddle

Published by Women Press. Los Angeles, CA.

Cover design by Pixel Studio.
Author photo by Caroline White.

First Printing, 2015

ISBN-13: 978-0692431450 (Women Press)
ISBN-10: 0692431454

Printed in the United States of America

For every woman and girl who has something to say . . .

Contents

An Invitation

This book is an invitation to all of you wise women who have a calling stirring in your heart and soul.

Who are tired of hiding, playing small, and keeping your big voice and big heart quiet.

Who feel a burning passion inside to be bigger, act bigger, and have more influence in the world.

Who want to stop apologizing for having an opinion, having a belief, having a vision of how things should be.

Who believe in the human rights of women and girls and want to take a stand for our liberation and self-realization.

Who seek to have a greater voice in the world so that you can be an active contributor to ending the cycles of war, poverty and violence.

This book is an invitation to the peacemakers, passion bearers, and creative expressionists among you.

I wrote this for you, dear Sister, whether you sit at a corporate desk, run your own business, star in a hit TV show, study as a student, balance motherhood with the rest of life, or simply have something to say – this is for you.

I invite you onto this journey to find your voice, embody your courage, and become the leader you were born to be.

The world is waiting for you . . .

INTRODUCTION

Here are the facts: Households headed by a female and women over 60 are the two poorest demographic groups in the United States. Women and children are 70 percent of the poor and 90 percent of those on welfare, and one in four mothers in the paid labor force is the sole support of her family.

Of all single mothers, nearly two-thirds are working in low-wage retail, service or administrative jobs that offer little flexibility, benefits or economic support to provide for or allow needed family time with their children.

All this is happening while women outnumber men at every level of higher education. (Women are earning almost 60 percent of undergraduate degrees, and 60 percent of all master's degrees.)

Globally, it gets worse. Women and children are two-thirds of the world's poor, 90 percent of the world's refugee populations, and adult women are two-thirds of the illiterate population because of lack of access to education.

One out of five of us will be raped or be a victim of attempted rape in our lifetime, and one out of three of us will be beaten, coerced into sex or otherwise abused by an intimate partner.

Women face discrimination and gender-based violence the world over, and it is time for this to stop.

***

I wasn't always so outspoken about women's rights. In fact, I didn't even have an awareness of all of these atrocities for a good deal of my life.

Like many women of my generation growing up in a middle-class or upper-middle class family, I was raised to believe that opportunities were open for me and that if I worked hard enough, I could do anything that a man could do.

On the outside, this seemed to be true. I was seeing women go into space, be appointed to the Supreme Court, run for Congress, become a Vice-Presidential candidate of the United States, anchor the news, work as lawyers, doctors, engineers and journalists. No one was talking about the dead ends women were running into because as far as most of us knew, they were busy breaking glass ceilings.

But something else was happening on a subtle level.

***

I used to feel that my voice didn't matter. I grew up as the youngest child and only girl in a family of two brothers, and a very strong lineage of male leaders going back to the earliest days of the United States.

My family came over with William Penn in the 1600s to escape religious persecution in England. My family was one of Philadelphia's early families, and while they were Quakers (who believe in non-violence), we have a healthy list of military leaders in our family history. This irony has never escaped me.

In addition to military leaders, we have a significant male lineage of ambassadors, politicians, diplomats and bank leaders, including my great-great-great grandfather who served as the President of the Second Bank of the United States under the administration of President James Monroe.

While there is a lot to be proud of in my family history, there is something very obvious that is missing. *The voices of women.*

I grew up under the shadow of my male lineage. While no one openly disparaged women in my immediate family as far as I could see, there was a subtle, and very potent, "betterness" equated to men and boys.

Like many girls and young women growing up in a patriarchal culture, I embodied this "less than" attitude and stance in the world as I grew up. While I was a leader in many regards through my sports teams, social groups, and academic strengths – there was still a shadow I was living under that, for a long time, I could not name.

***

I had an awakening nearly 10 years ago that changed everything.

I had recently moved from New York to Los Angeles, where I was working as a preschool teacher, when I started to get a distinct feeling that I needed to move beyond the four walls of the classroom and take my talents and abilities onto a wider platform. I had no idea what that meant at the time, but I trusted my intuition.

That spring, I decided not to renew my teaching contract – a bold move, since I didn't have another job lined up. All I knew was that whatever was next for me had to do with my "voice." At first, I thought I might have a singing career ahead of me. (I will mention here that this was not out of the question, since I had recently recorded a CD of children's music and was making the rounds as a singer at children's birthday parties.)

But what came next was a complete surprise. I had, what I call, "An Awakening to the Goddess."

I somehow got a direct line to Her. I know this might sound a bit strange (and believe me, I'm having trouble figuring out how to write to you about the experience), but what I can say about it is that I got a clear request to bring the Goddess out of the yoga studios and ashrams, and into mainstream culture.

Through this awakening, I became acutely aware of the human rights abuses of women and girls around the world (something I had turned a blind eye to previously), and began to feel intrinsically connected to all of the suffering that we have endured as the feminine part of the human race. I also became distinctly aware of how much we had been forced into a secondary position in society, and how devalued we were because of our gender.

The Goddess awakened me to the oppression of women's voices, the oppression of women's bodies, and ultimately the oppression of the feminine.

It became very clear to me that in order to ever achieve peace in our world — something that I had always believed was possible since I was a child, we needed to re-balance the masculine with the feminine, both within ourselves and within worldly leadership. I became clear, determined, and committed to playing my part in this evolution.

That's when I found my voice and began to actively speak out against discrimination and violence toward women. And that's when I discovered my greater purpose.

Now let's talk about yours.

YOUR DIVINE ASSIGNMENT

We all have a Divine Assignment. You may refer to this as your calling, your purpose, your dharma, your mission, your life's work, your service. Whatever you call it, it's ultimately about finding out what your unique purpose is here on earth so that you can get on track and fulfill your life's potential.

You can feel it when you are not aligned with your purpose. It aches. It frustrates. It exasperates. It saddens. It infuriates. We've all been there. You may be there right now. In fact, your Divine Assignment may be the very thing that has led you to pick up this book.

You may have found your way to this book because you want to align with your greater purpose and use your voice in the world, without apology or second-guessing; you may feel ready to take a stand and use your voice for what you believe in and what you value; and you most likely desire to move beyond the self-doubt that has been plaguing you for awhile, and move into a place of trusting yourself and your instincts.

I welcome you on this journey.

WHO YOU ARE

Let's talk about who you are, really, beyond your job title or what it says on your resume. Beneath the professional exterior you present to the world, you may be a creative entrepreneur, a corporate executive working to create change from the inside, a manager, a mother, an artist, an activist, a visionary, a student, a teacher, a healer, or simply a woman who wants to find her voice.

Some of you might be clear that you want to use your voice for social and political change, but you don't know where to start, and feel overwhelmed by the idea of going at this alone. I welcome you on the journey, and am here to help.

Most likely you have been on a path of personal growth for some time now, and are starting to feel a call to integrate your personal growth with social responsibility, social action and greater leadership.

What you share in common with each other, and I share with you, is a deep desire to express yourself, answer that calling inside of you, and become the leader you were born to be. Let's work together to accomplish that, and let's start with the best ways to use this book.

HOW TO USE THIS BOOK

I have designed this book to be both educational and inspiring, with experiential exercises and practices to help you find your voice and put your discoveries into action. You will need a few materials to support you as you read this book, which I describe below. You will also need a sacred space to do some of your practices.

I suggest reading this book in installments, allowing time to digest the content of each chapter and the discoveries you make in your practices. My suggestion would be to give yourself 14 days for the journey, reading a chapter a day, more or less. Giving yourself this clear, consistent container for the journey will benefit you greatly.

If you can, read the chapter at the same time each day (or a similar time) so that it becomes a daily ritual for you. You will need to set aside about 30 minutes for each chapter.

Connecting with a daily practice will help you listen deeply to your calling, and show up fully for your mission here on the planet.

Here is what you will need for your journey into leadership.

SACRED SPACE

Pick a place in your home that feels sacred to you. This is a place where you feel at ease; where you can be still and quiet; and where you won't get distracted by your to-do list. You may want to put a few special items around you that inspire you and help you drop deeper into yourself – creating an altar of sorts. (I know some of you already have altars, so this would be a great place to do your reading, experiential exercises and feminine leadership practices, which I will talk about shortly.)

VOICE JOURNAL

Throughout the next couple of weeks, we will be engaging in longhand, stream-of-consciousness writing. Journaling is one of the best ways to listen to your inner guidance. Your inner voice is asking to be heard. She just needs you to give her some unedited time in your journal. Every time you write in your journal, be curious about the wisdom coming through you and what your inner guidance has to say. The more you let yourself unwind in your journal, the more your own wisdom will be revealed to you. There is no wrong way to do this. You do not need to sound smart or clever. Nothing is too petty, silly, or stupid. Just let your pen flow.

I suggest picking out a brand new journal for this journey and taking a few moments in your sacred space to set an intention for this sacred container for your voice. Invite your journal to be a place of discovery, trust and deep friendship with yourself, so that you may unleash the true you, and follow the calling of your soul.

FEMININE LEADERSHIP PRACTICE

Many leadership books and programs out there today are still based on a masculine-oriented model, neglecting to honor and cultivate where a woman's true power comes from — being a woman. What makes this book and my leadership programs different is that I define leadership as something that is innate in every woman, and not necessarily something that needs to be learned, as much as it needs to be Remembered.

Before each journal exercise in the book, I offer you a feminine leadership practice. All of the practices are intended to reconnect you with your body, and to help you more easily access your intuition, wisdom and authentic voice. Doing these practices is an important step along the pathway of reclaiming your feminine authority and authentic voice. Please don't skip them.

***

I want to acknowledge that there are a lot of fears that can come up around becoming more visible as a feminine leader. I get it. I've been there, and I still constantly work on this and through this (you'll hear more about this later in the book), and so do so many of the clients in my leadership coaching practice. If you have some major fears around visibility, you are not alone, and we will be addressing this as we move forward.

My hope is that after reading this book you will feel absolutely clear about your purpose, confident and courageous about using your voice, and in full ownership of your feminine authority. My intention is for this book to give you the tools you need to boldly come forward in your leadership, trailblazing much-needed social and political change in the 21st century.

The world is waiting for you. So, let's get you on track and into action!

CHAPTER 1
Why You Need to Find Your Voice

"Don't think about making women fit the world – think about making the world fit women."

– Gloria Steinem

Deep inside of you there is a message waiting to be born into the world. Your inner voice is trying to speak to you. Can you hear Her?

Today there are so many of us who are feeling a calling deep inside to change the world in a *big* way. We feel it in our hearts. We feel it in our souls. We feel it in our bones. We feel it in our body and breath.

All too often though we have run away from this calling because we are scared of the *bigness* of it. We are scared to reveal ourselves as being that grand. We are scared to stand in the spotlight, be visible, and maybe most of all, scared to stand out and be the one who rocks the status quo.

We grew up in a male-dominated culture that taught women and girls that our voice doesn't matter. Or, if we were lucky enough to be told otherwise, it was always with the backdrop of being secondary to men.

Our culture taught us it was better to keep quiet, be polite, and assume the role of the "good girl."

In this position, our opinions were not valued and our emotions were not invited. In those moments when we did allow our emotions to be expressed, all too often we were ridiculed. Consequently, we learned to clamp down on our self-expression, abandon how we truly feel, and mute our truth.

This is how our authentic voices became silenced, lost even to ourselves.

***

Today, women's knowledge, wisdom and opinions are woefully underrepresented around the world. In every country and in every industry, women are undervalued, underpaid and often completely missing from positions of power and authority.

In the United States, we represent just 19 percent of our elected government, just 16 percent of corporate boards, just 16 percent of all directors, executive producers, writers, cinematographers and editors in Hollywood, just three percent of top decision-making positions in the media; and in religious leadership, we are practically invisible.

Globally, women represent just one in every five parliamentarians. The United States, by the way, ranks 60th in women's political empowerment, according to a study by the Center for American Progress.

This is a big problem for us personally and for the world.

On the personal level, our voices are absent in addressing the issues that most affect our lives and the lives of our children. Instead of leading the public conversation with our values, beliefs and life experiences, we are following it. Hence, what matters to us most never gets to the table.

Furthermore, on a personal level, if we don't express ourselves fully, there can be mental and emotional health repercussions, later leading to physical disease. All too common for women.

Women's health specialist and author of *Women's Bodies, Women's Wisdom*, Christiane Northrup, M.D., says that many illnesses are quite simply the end result of emotions that have been stuffed, unacknowledged and unexperienced for years. "Unexpressed emotions tend to 'stay' in the body like small ticking time bombs," she says. "They are illnesses in incubation."

In addition to our own health risks, stuffing our emotions and opinions and keeping our voices quiet have consequences for our planet.

As my friend and colleague, Dr. Marcy Cole, Ph.D., a licensed clinical social worker in Los Angeles, puts it: "Women are natural nurturers, healers, intuitives, creators, visionaries and peacemakers. When we dis-empower ourselves by withholding our voices, we ignore the call for feminine leadership that is absolutely crucial for this planet at this time."

I couldn't agree more.

You see, a woman's voice is the vehicle through which her wisdom is transmitted. When women's wisdom is absent, war, poverty, oppression and violence are the name of the game. Aggression, competition, and power over, rather than *power with,* are the norm.

But we, as women, know that this is not a natural way of living.

We believe in peace, collaboration, compassion, connection, community and taking care of the human beings on this earth.

We believe in loving and honoring our planet and taking care of Her resources. We believe in honoring human dignity and the preciousness of life. We know that violence does not solve conflicts, and only breeds more violence and hatred in the world.

But since our voices are silenced and absent in most leadership circles, we remain in the unnatural spin cycle of war, poverty and violence. Without our feminine voice, the world spins out of balance.

This absence of women's wisdom and the truth of women's lives translates into laws, public policy, and resource distribution that don't accurately reflect the needs, wants and desires of women and, in turn, our children and future generations. For this reason, women and girls continue to suffer both at home and abroad.

***

The good news is that you have the power in you right now to change this. As you find the courage to honor the truth of your feminine voice and use your voice more visibly and publicly, you will enact change.

Your inner voice is trying to speak to you. Can you hear Her?

When you embark on the path of finding, or rediscovering, your voice, you will find a well of wisdom probably way beyond what you could have ever imagined. You will start to feel more *alive*, more purposeful, driven, motivated, excited, passionate, invigorated, creative, decisive and on purpose. And maybe most delightfully, you will get to touch and taste the immense power of you.

The moment you stop believing that others have more valuable opinions than you, and that your voice doesn't matter, everything changes.

Let's get started.

Try this:

FEMININE LEADERSHIP PRACTICE

Remember when I told you that I define leadership as something that is innate in every woman, and something that doesn't necessary need to be learned, as much as it needs to be Remembered? Now we are going to put that into practice.

All of the feminine leadership practices that I offer in this book are intended to reconnect you with your body (a powerful source of your feminine wisdom) and your natural spiritual authority. As you do these practices, you will Remember who you are as a woman and will remember your innate leadership qualities. Doing these practices will be a pathway to you reclaiming your feminine leadership and authority.

You'll see that I invite you to set a timer for a lot of these exercises and that the times are short. That is because I want you to go with instinctive responses and not labor over this. Trust your intuition.

Step into your sacred space. Set a timer for 2 minutes.

Womb Breathing. As a woman, your womb is the storehouse of your feminine wisdom. Without a deep awareness of and relationship with your womb, it is difficult to align with your authentic voice and your life's purpose. Take 2 minutes for this empowerment practice to tune into your womb, get into your body and open up the channels for you to be able to more easily receive and access the wisdom coming through you.

- Start with closing your eyes and dropping your attention inward.

- Draw your attention and your breath down to your womb area. If it helps, you can place your hands on your belly and womb.

- First, give thanks for being a woman and give gratitude for the deep feminine mysteries and wisdom that are held within your body.

- Second, acknowledge that everything you need to know is actually encoded in your body, and that I am just a voice today to help you REMEMBER who you are and help you awaken to the wisdom that is already held within you.

- Set an intention to be willing to "see" and "hear" the voice of your feminine wisdom today and to honor Her with an open heart and open arms.

- Receive your breath through your *entire* body. Move your hands up to your heart, then to your throat and neck, now give yourself a cheek, jaw and mouth massage, and then loosen up your tongue and lips with possibly some silly sounds, depending where you are, then give yourself a refreshing mini-head and hair massage.

- Finish on an exhale. And then slowly open your eyes.

FIND YOUR VOICE INTERVIEW

Take out your journal and a pen. Set a timer for 1 minute for each question. Answer each question in a stream-of-consciousness way. Do not edit yourself. Keep your pen to paper the whole time and keep writing from your intuitive self. Let the words flow, and tell your inner critic to take a vacation, just for the time it takes to do this interview exercise. Save your answers. We will be using your responses for some upcoming leadership work.

1. What do you see happening in the world that feels unjust?

2. What is the change you want to see in the world?

3. Who are the people you want to help?

EX: open up the channels
ask Qs to find xsonal
mission

CHAPTER 2
Your Responsibility as a Woman

"You have the responsibility to be lights because that's who you really are."

– Maya Angelou

I once read in a Gloria Steinem essay that eating disorders literally starve females out of all sexual characteristics – from breasts to menstruation – and are almost totally restricted to social groups in which the "feminine" role itself is the most restrictive. She said it's as if the young women look at the "dependent, decorative, lesser, ladylike role that awaits them," and unconsciously starve themselves out of it.

As a young girl, I grew up spending summers in Rhode Island where all of our cousins, aunts, uncles and grandparents would flock. We were all from Philadelphia, originally.

I had a set of friends who I would see once a year during this summertime season. My best friend was Katherine[1]. She was six months younger than me.

Katherine and I spent our days sailing, swimming, playing tennis and biking. We were active and on the go. We loved playing all day long. We did this for years together.

---

[1]Some names used in this book have been changed to protect privacy.

This changed abruptly one summer. We were 13 years old.

One afternoon I arrived over at Katherine's house on my bike expecting to go for our usual ride to the beach. To my surprise, Katherine didn't want to go.

I questioned her. Goaded her. Tried to motivate her. Begged her. But she didn't want to go.

Why doesn't she want to go with me to the beach? This is what we do! I felt sad, betrayed, and confused.

Her mom saw the discomfort Katherine felt, with no voice to explain herself, and stepped in to tell me: "Katherine has her period, and she doesn't want to go to the beach."

Her period??????!!! What????!!!!!

I wasn't ready for this. I wasn't ready for my best friend to become a woman. I wasn't ready for my best friend to have breasts (which she had miraculously grown over the year I hadn't seen her). I wasn't ready for any of this. I don't know if Katherine was either.

Our friendship changed that summer. Instead of palling around on the tennis courts and riding our bikes around town, I was learning about Katherine's Weight Watchers diet. With the onset of womanhood, my once tiny friend had put on a significant amount of weight and she and her mother felt a special diet would be the best thing for her.

She was 13 and on a Weight Watchers diet.

If it could happen to her, it could happen to me. And you better believe that I wasn't going to let it happen.

That fall I went back to Philadelphia and started my freshman year of high school. The year started out strong – seeing my friends, playing on the field hockey team, loving my English class, and dating a "junior" boy from the football team.

But by late fall things were starting to change.

Having gotten turned on to Katherine's Weight Watchers' menu over the summer, I started to implement some of these food choices into my routine. Alba milkshakes for breakfast. Wasa crackers for lunch. Salads for dinner and fat-free fudge popsicles for dessert. Along with this, I started to skip a breakfast here, and a lunch there. My energy started to wane and I noticed I wasn't being as social as I typically was with my friends.

I was becoming anorexic, but no one seemed to notice.

My mom and brothers certainly hadn't said anything, and neither had my friends. This was the 1980s, so wearing over-sized clothes was in, but in retrospect I don't think the baggy clothes could ultimately disguise my weight loss.

Like many young women with an eating disorder, my new-found eating habits helped me to feel "in control" at a time when I felt that life around me was very out of control. My friends and I were experimenting with drinking and dating older boys, and I was living in a single-parent home with my mom and one of my brothers. My other brother was off at college. My mom also had a boyfriend, which meant she was out a lot more than I was used to.

The idea that I would also have to transition into having hips and boobs and my period at this time was beyond me. I felt that if I became a "woman" I would lose my entire identity of who I considered myself to be – an athletic, smart, pretty, tom-boy type. Girl pretty was okay to me. Woman pretty was a whole other can of worms.

And so, my stalling technique worked. Whatever boobs I had disappeared as my weight slipped away. I had no hips. And I had yet to get my period.

Success! (Or so I thought.)

Over the course of six months, I went from 5 feet 6 inches tall and 125 pounds to 5 feet 6 inches tall and 98 pounds. Not a healthy weight for a growing teenager, as you might imagine.

While I was working so hard to fight off losing my identity as a girl, I was actually losing myself in a much bigger way. I didn't know who I was anymore.

Once the popular, out-going girl, I began to slip between the cracks. I was withdrawing from my friends, initially turning down social invitations, then eventually not receiving them at all.

I was confused and alone. *What had gone wrong? How could I ever find my way back?*

My answer came in the form of a friend. She was my best friend from childhood in Philadelphia. She lived next door and was a year older than me.

One afternoon I stepped out of the shower and into my room and found her waiting for me. I hadn't spent any time with her in months since our social groups were quite different now that we were teenagers. She was in the tenth grade, while I was only a freshman.

She looked at me in horror and said: "What have you done to yourself!?"

I was embarrassed, ashamed, and also, in a sense, relieved. I knew exactly what she meant. Someone had *finally* noticed. I was not alone anymore. My secret was no longer a secret.

This began my road to recovery. Soon after, my mom booked a doctor "check-up" appointment for me. This is how it was presented to me, at least.

This is where my condition was addressed head on. Alone in the office with the doctor, he told me that my mom was concerned about me, and he asked me if I thought I was "fat."

Fat? Is he kidding me? No way! I'm tiny. I'm wasting away here.

So it was clear that I did not have that aspect of

anorexia.

He said we needed to have a plan to get my weight back up. I promised to eat normally and to not skip meals. He was skeptical, and prescribed me some weight-gaining protein milkshakes to get things started.

I kept my promise. Within five months, I was back up to close to where I started. A few months after that, I got my period. And when I got it, I was actually proud. I could feel that there was something very special to this feminine power. Womanhood started to look different.

***

I need to talk about my entire sexual history story

I share this story with you because I think it captures the ambivalence and, in some cases, deep resistance that many girls go through when they are approaching womanhood. You may have experienced this to some degree yourself.

Whether conscious or otherwise, as a girl approaches womanhood, she sees that womanhood does not afford her the same freedoms she had as a girl. Now she has to be prepared for the potential of unwanted sexual attention, sexual harassment and sexual assault. She may now have to cover up her body, alter her posture, and stifle her physical expression to keep herself protected.

She may also have hopes and dreams that are now not considered "a realistic path" or "appropriate choices" for a woman, but may have seemed just fine for a girl.

The world starts to look different through the lens of a woman.

***

As girls grow and develop, their sense of self-esteem and personal worth change too. Studies show that by age 15, *X*

[Not that 1 in 5 women have sex. distinction — but that society is fucked up!]

21

girls are twice as likely as boys to become depressed.

Their changing bodies and changing social roles all too often become a place of confusion and, at the same time, an overwhelming measure of their worth. Self-esteem unfortunately becomes tied to physical appearance and sexual appeal, with the aspirational standards set by the media, which by the way, is mostly run by men.

In movies, television, music videos, video games, magazines, advertisements, billboards and on the Internet, women and girls are hyper-sexualized. This is a mixed message for girls. *dsn't teach girls to say no when in dangerous situations*

How can I be a "good girl" and be popular at the same time? How can I express who I am becoming, while not bringing on unwanted sexual attention? How can I have the freedoms I did as a girl even though I'm now a woman?

According to the American Psychological Association, the sexualization of girls in media undermines a girl's confidence in and comfort with her own body, leading to anxiety, shame and difficulty in developing a healthy sexual self-image.

Not surprisingly, sexualization of girls has been linked to eating disorders, low self-esteem and major depression (the most common mental health problem amongst women and girls).

Even among young women who have been valedictorians in their high schools, studies show that their intellectual self-esteem tends to diminish with every year of higher education.

Interestingly, young men's self-esteem goes up over their four years of college.

One factor likely contributing to this conundrum is that many young women have absorbed the idea that they have to be "twice as good" in order to be taken half as seriously as men. Simultaneously, they are criticized and shamed for exhibiting "too much" ambition, often earning them the titles of "pushy," "bossy" or "bitchy."

A little confusing, right?

There's also the element of social standards where a young woman is expected to be smart, popular, beautiful and fit – all while making it look effortless. At the same time she is expected to listen to and laugh at the sexist jokes being made by her male peers (and maybe even her professors), and be exposed to a culture of rape where one in four of her friends, or her, will be the victim of sexual assault during her four years in college. And when this crime is reported, she will most likely not get the legal support she needs to bring her abuser to justice. Alternatively, what she will get is victim blaming and shaming around her sexuality.

Or maybe it's the fact that in her college textbooks she sees fewer and fewer women, and all of those promises made to her when she was a girl about being anything she wanted to be start to get chipped away. So much so that she doesn't really know where her place is in society anymore and where to focus her brilliance.

***

One of the best ways to break this cycle of oppression is to encourage girls and young women to speak their minds. And how can we best do this?

By speaking our own minds.

When girls see women in leadership roles speaking out for what they believe in, they see it is possible for them too. They see that what women have to say is important and therefore start to value their own voice. Instead of a faraway dream, their aspirations become real, concrete and achievable.

Womanhood starts to look more inviting.

In the words of Marian Wright Edelman, founder and president of the Children's Defense Fund, "You can't be what you can't see." While I do believe young women can break new ground, create and achieve what has never been seen, I think a culture of women speaking up and speaking out about what they believe in is essential to this momentum.

It is in your hands.

As the keepers of feminine wisdom and feminine trailblazers of the 21st century, it is our responsibility to regain our confidence and worthiness around our voice. No one else can do this for us.

Katie Orenstein, founder of the The OpEd Project, shared her thoughts on this in an interview with me, saying, "There are people who narrate the world, who own history, who own the story. And there are people who are characters in the story. The story never reflects very well the needs or perspectives of those who aren't telling it. If you are not the one telling your story, it's not being told the way you would tell it."

The OpEd Project is an initiative to expand the range of voices and quality of ideas we hear in the world, with a specific focus on increasing the number of women thought leaders contributing to influential commentary forums. I have been greatly inspired by their work and am an alumni of their "Find Your Voice: Change the World" program.

Each time you step up and say something or do something that breaks the silence, oppression or limiting cultural perspective of women, you do it for all the girls and young women that follow.

By increasing the number of female role models, we can

begin to alter the global perception of women.

Our generation of women is clearing the path for our daughters, granddaughters, women and girls down the line, to feel safe to be the woman or girl that they are – and to be fully self-expressed in their full feminine fortitude.

The world is aching for feminine wisdom to come forward. The world is starving for feminine compassion, connection and community. The world is begging for you, as a woman, to step forward with your voice so that you can contribute to the healing of humanity and our planet.

This is your responsibility as a woman.

tell the story

Control the gaze

Elizabeth Kilpatrick
and ?? ??
(right hand of Geena Davis)

Try this:

FEMININE LEADERSHIP PRACTICE

Step into your sacred space. Set a timer for 2 minutes.

Take up space. As women, we have all too often made ourselves small in order to not "step on anyone's toes," "be too loud," "be too much," or call in unwanted sexual attention. This has literally made some of us collapse in our very own bodies. Our shoulders hunch, our posture folds, and we feel tightly held in space. Our body posture becomes a metaphor for how we show up in the world. For many of us, it's the "I'm sorry" epidemic that we carry around just for being a woman. Now is the season to change this.

- Stand with your feet wider than hip's distance apart. Ground them firmly into the earth.

- Stretch out your arms, shoulder height, as far as you can on both the left and right sides. Spread your fingers on each hand.

- Reach your fingertips out as far as you can on both the right and left side. Keep your feet grounded.

- Feel your chest, heart and solar plexus open. Breathe.

- Remain in this space-taking, outstretched position for 1 minute. Breathe.

- Notice the sensations coming up as you take up space. Don't change a thing. Just note them.

- Allow your heart to smile, your throat to open, and your eyes to focus. Breathe.

- When the timer sounds, bring your hands to your heart and bow your head in gratitude for the magnificence of who you are. Say out loud: "I am a magnificent woman, deserving of taking up space with my voice, my body and my presence."

FIND YOUR VOICE INTERVIEW

Take out your journal and a pen. Set a timer for 1 minute for each question. Answer each question in a stream-of-consciousness way. Do not edit yourself. Remember to tell your inner critic to take a vacation. Keep your pen to paper the whole time and write from your intuitive self. Save your answers. We will be using your responses for some upcoming leadership work.

1. Take a moment to envision yourself taking the stage and speaking to a group of girls or young women. What do you see yourself talking to them about? What wisdom or life experiences do you have to share that could help them?

2. By the end of your talk, how do you want them to feel? And what do you want them to do?

3. How do you feel about being a woman?

CHAPTER 3
✗✗ Do Not Be Afraid of Your Power

"Women have to be taught that ambition is ladylike."

– Nancy Pelosi

D o you ever wonder if you sometimes keep yourself small because you are afraid of your actual power? Do you ever wonder if you keep yourself small so that you will be "likeable" and not mistaken for a "bitch"? Do you ever wonder what it would be like to actually own your power?

It's no secret that we have been socialized to fear women's power, to view it as something negative, something unattractive, something unlikeable.

When Sheryl Sandberg, COO of Facebook, was doing research in 2010 for her now-famous TED talk, "Why We Have Too Few Women Leaders," she came across a striking social pattern: When women are in positions of power and are ambitious, assertive and successful in their work, they are often labeled as aggressive, bitchy or unlikable, whereas a man exhibiting the same qualities is seen as confident and likeable.

"Success and likeability are positively correlated for men and negatively correlated for women," said Sheryl in her talk. In other words – he's a boss, and she's a bitch. It was somewhat shocking to hear this spoken out loud back in 2010. Now, even though it is discussed openly, the problem remains deep, and a remedy hard to come by.

This is a real trap for most of us women because we care about being liked. In fact, our brains are wired for this.

According to Louann Brizendine, M.D., a neurobiologist and psychiatrist at the University of California, our distinct female biology provides an explanation of why we are so focused on gaining acceptance from others.

It turns out that compared to the male brain, the female brain has a larger communication center and a larger area for processing emotion and reading social cues, therefore leaving women and girls more emotionally sensitive than men and more aware of social disapproval.

In her bestselling book, *The Female Brain*, Dr. Brizendine explains that because baby girls are born interested in emotional expression, they take meaning about themselves from a look, a touch, every reaction from the people they come into contact with. "From these cues they decide whether they are worthy, lovable or annoying," says Dr. Brizendine.

She goes on to say: "Whether or not she is being listened to will tell a young girl if others take her seriously, which in turn goes to the growth of her sense of a successful self. If she does not connect, her sense is of an unsuccessful self," says Dr. Brizendine.

This makes it pretty clear why the female race spends so much of our time trying to be liked.

The result, however, can be detrimental.

Feminist writer Jessica Valenti explored this dilemma in a 2012 essay in *The Nation* titled, "She Who Dies with the Most 'Likes' Wins?" In it, she discusses the countless hours she wasted arguing with people on the Internet, giving equal time to thoughtful and asinine commenters, all in an effort to show herself to be fair and open-minded. She laments over what she could have achieved if she had used that precious time for other purposes.

"Women adjust their behavior to be likeable and as a result have less power in the world," she said.

It's true. Remember all of those times you tempered your words because you didn't want to offend, silenced your opinion because you didn't want to challenge the status quo, or agonized over choosing the right words to write on social media because you wanted to be "liked." Did that feel powerful?

"Wanting to be liked means being a supporting character in your own life, using the cues of the actors around you to determine your next line rather than your own script. It means that your self-worth will always be tied to what someone else thinks about you, forever out of your control," says Jessica.

That's definitely not a place of power.

While we can't rewire our brains, we can stop this cultural pattern of demonizing and disparaging women's power by changing the direction of the conversation.

How do we do this?

***

The first thing we need to do is acknowledge that there is a problem. We need to acknowledge that we have been made to fear our own power.

We can share our experiences of this in women's circles, write about this in our blogs, make media about this, and create art. We can take this reality out from the shadows and shine a light on it so it no longer unconsciously controls us.

Secondly, we need to hold media accountable for how they are treating women leaders. We can comment on their

30

online platforms, write letters to the editor, Tweet about it, and make our own media about it.

Thirdly, we can celebrate women in power and women in general. Talk about them. Write about them. Make media about them. Make art of and about them.

And finally, we can embody and stand in our own power. As we do this, we set the stage and clear the path for the women and girls following us in the coming generations. As Jessica Valenti wrote in *The Nation*, "And saying that ambition and success are actually pretty great can be a radical message" to deliver to women and girls.

This social change – valuing, respecting and encouraging women's power – can only come about when we women speak up and stand up for ourselves and what we believe in, and support our sisters in doing the same. All the while, cheering them on for being opinionated, outspoken and assertive.

It is up to us to find our voice. Trust our own authority. And stand up for what we believe in. That is how we create change.

I want to acknowledge again that there are a lot of fears that can come up around standing up for what we believe in and becoming more visible as a feminine leader.

Patriarchal society has worked very hard to keep women and girls down and separate from our own power. The media have played a great hand in this with programming that offers a negative portrayal of women and sends a clear cultural message that women are not equal.

According to research commissioned by the Geena Davis Institute on Gender in Media, the more hours of television a girl watches, the fewer career options she thinks she has because media is not showing that women have a leadership role in society.

In G-rated family films made from 2006 to 2009, research revealed that 80 percent of all characters who held jobs were male. And of the 20 percent of working characters that were female, not one was depicted in the fields of medical science, law, politics or as a business leader.

This is in strong contrast to real world statistics, where women comprise 50 percent of the workforce.

Add to this that the percentage of females with speaking roles in top-grossing movies has not meaningfully changed in roughly half of a century, and when they do have roles, they are often gender-stereotyped and hyper-sexualized.

Much of this has to do with the fact that females are underrepresented behind the camera as well.

A study titled *Gender Disparity Behind the Camera in Family Films* revealed that in a group of over 1,500 Hollywood content creators, only seven percent of directors, 13 percent of writers, and 20 percent of producers were female.

This translates to five times the number of men creating, telling the stories and providing the lens and cultural perspective that girls and boys grow up on.

It is clear that we need more women in the creative process driving the content. Perhaps then girls will see their options open up and feel encouraged to express their power.

But in order for all these things to happen, we need to step into our own leadership *sooner rather than later*. We need to go through the dark alleys, the dark shadows, and some of the other places we have been resistant to encountering, in order to make it to the other side.

It is your time to reclaim your power, be proud of your

power, and speak out for what you believe in.

It is your time to contribute to ending the cultural pattern of negating, vilifying, and separating women from their power.

Let's do this.

Try this:

FEMININE LEADERSHIP PRACTICE

Step into your sacred space. Set a timer for 3 minutes.

Pelvis Power. As women, our pelvis and hips are a great storehouse of our power. This is the place from which we give birth (both literally and figuratively). In order to access this power, we need to remove blockages or stagnancy and awaken the hips and pelvis by creating a safe and fun relationship with them. Set your timer for 3 minutes for this practice.

- Sit comfortably in your sacred space breathing easily for 1 minute.

- Slowly transition to your feet.

- Take your feet slightly wider than the width of your hips and bend your knees slightly.

- Start to let your hands explore your hips. Feel the curves. Feel their texture.

- Give your hips a gentle massage. Do they feel relaxed? Do they feel tight? Do they feel excited? Do they feel agitated? Try not to judge. Just be curious.

- Place your hands gently on your hips and start taking your hips in a circle. Keep your knees soft.

- For 1 minute, keep moving your hips in one direction. How do they feel? How do *you* feel? Notice if anything is coming up for you. Then let yourself simply sink into the movement.

- After a minute, change the circle to the other direction. This direction might feel different for you. Be curious about it.

- Start to let your hands and arms flow freely, allowing them to express however they'd like to.

- Start to let your hips and pelvis move however they want to (big, small, spiral, in one direction or the other . . .). Let your hips express themselves. Invite your hips to move in any way that feels delicious for them. If your hips don't take the lead, you can take the lead and then slowly ask your hips to guide you. Just focus on being in your body.

- After a minute, ask your hips and pelvis: "What do you want to say?" Listen closely and follow their guidance. The response might come in the form of movement, it might come in the form of words, or it might come in both forms. Be curious and keep moving.

- Continue luxuriating in your hips and pelvis for another minute or so, and then gradually come to stillness. Close your eyes and feel your breath move through your body. Enjoy the stillness, and feel what's alive in your body.

FIND YOUR VOICE INTERVIEW

Take out your journal and a pen. Set a timer for 1 minute for each question. Answer each question in a stream-of-consciousness way. Do not edit yourself. Keep your pen to paper the whole time and write from your intuitive self. Save your answers. We will be using your responses for some upcoming leadership work.

1. Take a moment to see yourself on stage, embodied in your most powerful self. In this state, what message would you be sharing?

2. In this state, how does your body want to express itself?

3. What is the change you feel you are being called to create in the world?

The World is Waiting

You are a woman leader. You feel it deep inside.

You have taken steps to become more vocal

More visible

Less apologetic for who you are and what you stand for.

You have watched yourself expand in your leadership, and you have felt

Proud.

Exhilarated.

Hopeful.

But there are those moments when you falter.

You lose your footing.

You get overwhelmed.

You begin to doubt.

You ask the questions:

Who am I to do this?

Say this?

Change this?

Yet there is a voice within you that keeps beating

Keeps pumping

Keeps whispering . . .

GO FURTHER. GO FURTHER.

The world is waiting . . .

CHAPTER 4
Activating Your Political Voice

"We don't just need new policies, we need a new world view."

– Marianne Williamson

I'm aware that the word "political" might bring up the heebie jeebies for some of you. It may not be a word that you feel warmly about or even connected to. It might make some of you want to run in the other direction, or maybe immediately exclude yourself from the conversation. You may have a bad taste in your mouth about politics and see it as divisive, corrupt and dirty.

I have heard this from many women, and for a time, I felt this way myself.

I know, however, that if you are reading this book you feel stirred to be a changemaker in some way and you most likely have a greater social mission sitting inside of you.

So I'm going to ask you to stay with me in this chapter.

What I want to propose is that it is important for you, as an emerging feminine changemaker, to create a new and different relationship with the word "political" – one where you get to redefine it for yourself so that you can do your greater work in the world.

My Political Awakening

I was 18 years old, sitting in a lecture hall with 150 other first-year college students in Waterville, Maine. The year was 1988 and the class was *Government 101*. There were three teachers on stage. All men.

I signed up for the class because I knew *nothing* about government. My parents weren't political, my brothers weren't political, and I didn't have any friends who were political.

I was an English major.

Up until that point, my only political experience that I could remember was in the fifth grade when I helped my classmate and her father canvass the neighborhood with campaign materials for a local candidate the father supported for City Council. That was it.

So here I was in this lecture hall taking a leap into a completely new topic for me. I was giddy and excited. I could feel that something important was about to happen.

The three teachers took the stage and introduced themselves. I liked them. They were animated and friendly. They seemed to have an ease, openness and warmth that I hadn't yet found in my other professors. I was drawn to listen and learn from them.

In that class, on that first day, they told me that I have a voice, and that my voice matters in our government. They told me that as a citizen of American democracy, not only did my vote count, but my voice mattered.

No one had ever told me that my voice mattered.

By the end of the second class, I went to see my college advisor in the English department and told him that I wanted to change my major to Government. I was taking a new path.

***

Like so many girls of my generation and upper-middle-class status, I had been taught that I could have a job and earn my own money. But I had never been taught that what I had to say was actually valuable. I especially had never been taught that I could influence the laws and public policies that governed our country. My Mom was sitting on the sidelines during the feminist movement of the late 1960s and 70s. She told me, when I interviewed her for this book, that she was too shy at that time to be politically active, and she also felt that her voice didn't matter.

For these reasons, I thought government was something "done to me," as opposed to something I could influence.

This class changed my perspective.

As I stepped on the political path, I figured out pretty quickly that I was a Democrat. I joined the college Democrat Club and dove into organizing food drives and clothing drives for the underserved local community, and also embarked on learning the ins and outs of working on a political campaign.

I got to put my campaign skills into practice when our Democrat Club signed on to support the Congressional campaign of State Senator Tom Andrews (D-Maine), who was running for the U.S. House of Representatives. We canvassed. We worked the phone banks. We registered voters. State Senator Andrews even came to meet with us a couple of times on campus.

Before I knew it, I was the Vice President of the Democrat Club and was applying for internships in Washington, D.C., for my spring term of junior year. My focus was political journalism.

To my luck (and strong qualifications), I was accepted for an internship at the Washington bureau of CNN, working in the political division.

My assignment was to read five of the top-tier newspapers every day, including *The Washington Post*, *The*

Washington Times, The New York Times, The Wall Street Journal and *USA Today,* and clip all the major political stories. These were then later used by the political correspondents as background for their on-air reports.

I loved this kind of work as I felt like I was part of the action.

I even got to write, edit, produce, and be the on-air talent for my very own two-minute political "package." I covered how the Gulf War would affect the upcoming presidential election. (The First Gulf War – Operation Desert Storm – had broken out during my time at CNN.)

Back on campus my senior year, I resumed my position as Vice President of the Democrat Club, and worked with the group to bring influential politicians to our college campus to inspire the students to get involved in politics. Our guests included '92 presidential hopeful and current Secretary of State John Kerry, '92 presidential hopeful and current Governor of California Jerry Brown, Democratic candidate for the U.S. House of Representatives Tom Andrews, and wife of '92 presidential hopeful Bill Clinton and former Secretary of State Hillary Clinton.

When the president of our Democrat Club stepped down to move to the state capital of Maine to help run Bill Clinton's campaign in the state, guess who became president of the club?

Believe me, I had no idea when I entered college that I would become the President of the Democrat Club and be hosting presidential candidates on my campus.

Once on this path, though, I kept going.

Right after college, I moved back to Washington, D.C., and got a job working for the Women's Campaign Fund, an organization that supported pro-choice women running for political office. This is where I got a taste of what it takes to run a national campaign.

That year – 1992 – was seen as a successful one for women in office as the number of women in the U.S. Senate doubled (from two to four), and the number of women in Congress increased from 28 to 47, giving 1992 the so-called title, "Year of the Woman."

Once that election cycle was over, I needed to figure out my next step. One obvious consideration was the White House.

Having worked on the Clinton campaign when I was in Maine, I got myself a position on President Clinton's inaugural committee in Washington, working as a radio reporter. This gave me entry to the possibility of working for his administration.

It looked like I was on a clear path to working in the White House.

While I was a huge fan of President Clinton's platform and was heavily considering pursuing a job in his administration, my heart was leading me elsewhere.

I looked at the people ahead of me in politics and thought to myself: *Do I want to be like them?* The answer came swiftly.

NO.

***

I took a path away from politics because I didn't like the divisiveness of the political community. The environment was such that, because I was a Democrat, it was look upon badly for me to associate with Republicans. There was a bitter relationship between the two parties. Although I had met some great women through my work at the Women's Campaign Fund, I felt that the political atmosphere overall, and those who worked within it, were too cutthroat for me.

When I looked ahead to those in office, those were not the people who I wanted to emulate.

I was more smitten with the world travelers – the writers, photographers and documentary makers of world culture – helping us learn about each other, rather than separate us.

So where did I end up for the next four years?

At the National Geographic Society.

**

Perhaps you've had a similar experience with politics, put off by the rancor and divisiveness that is all too often present, especially evident during these last two sessions of Congress. While I stepped away for these reasons many years ago, I now see a different path for creating political change.

Let me show you.

Redefining Politics from a Feminine Perspective

I have come to realize that having a political voice does not mean you need to run for office. Although you could. It also does not mean that you have to lead rallies and demonstrations, or organize town halls. But you could.

What it does mean is that you are using your voice *anywhere you are* in a way that represents what you believe in, what you value, and what you stand for.

You see, the personal is political.

Remember this catchphrase of the women's movement of the late 1960s and 70s? There's a good reason for it. The changes that you want in your personal life *are* political.

For example, do you wish that you were making the same high salary as the man down the hall from you who is doing *the same work* as you? Or maybe you wish that you were not skipped over for the promotion for having a baby?

Do you wish that your spouse would play more of a role in parenting, but since he makes the higher salary, his job is considered "more valuable" and therefore you get overloaded with doing most of the housework and most of the parenting, on top of your full-time job?

Maybe you want to know that, if you were ever sexually harassed at work, on the street, at church, or even at your child's school, you are legally in the right to press charges and that the offender would be brought to justice.

Perhaps you wish that you lived in a society that did not tolerate physical, sexual or emotional abuse of women and girls. I know I do.

You see, your relationships, your role in the workplace, your income, your role in marriage, your feelings on motherhood, your feelings about your sexuality, and your personal safety are inseparable from the larger social and political structures that exist.

But right now, so many women's political voices are silenced because too many of us don't think we even have one. This is what we need to change, and *are* changing. You are doing the work right here, right now, as you read this book.

The feminine political voice, I believe, is personal. It's intimate. It's caregiving and life enhancing. It's about bringing more love, caring and justice into the world.

It's also fierce and determined. It's about providing opportunities for the underserved, the neglected, and the "invisible." It's about ending violence by solving conflict with communication, compassion and cooperation. It's about speaking our truth and sharing our life experiences.

As the prevailing voices in the public spotlight are predominantly men, stepping into the spotlight with the truth of who you are as a woman *is* political change.

Getting Clear on Your Political Vision

Okay, so how do you get clear on your political vision? And how do you articulate it?

Let's first shake some old conditioning out of your system. Let's shake out the socialization that told you that politics is not for you if you don't want a career in office, don't know any legislative lingo, or have never been on Capitol Hill.

I want to give you a moment right now to do just that. Shake your arms, legs, head, hips and every part of you that is still holding onto that old paradigm. Shake it out now.

Feels good, right?

Next, I want to check in with you about something. Do you remember the Find Your Voice Interview questions I asked you at the end of Chapters 1, 2 and 3?

I hope so, because guess what? Your responses to those questions are *your political vision.* Those personal questions I asked you were prompts to help you lay the foundation for articulating your political vision.

If you can't remember what you said in your responses, open up your journal right now and look back to remind yourself.

I'm going to take you through an exercise in a moment to help you get comfortable with articulating your political vision. This exercise can be done in private and is just for you. It will help you build courage, confidence and clarity in yourself and your ideals, and will pave the way for some of the more public work we are building to later in the book.

Are you in?

Articulating Your Political Vision

Pull out your Voice Journal and do a quick review of your responses to the interview questions from Chapters 1, 2 and 3. Find a quiet, private spot in your home, office or somewhere in nature and take a minute to sit and breathe. After you've centered yourself, come to your feet and place your feet hips-distance apart. Answer these questions aloud.

What do you see right now going on in the world that feels unjust?

(In your private space, speak this aloud.)

What is the change you would like to see in the world?

(Speak this aloud.)

What is the change you are feeling called to make in the world?

(Speak this aloud.)

Who are the people who will benefit from your calling? And how?

(Speak this aloud.)

***

You did it! You should feel proud of yourself for taking this action. Your words have power. When you speak things aloud, you make your vision concrete and that much closer to happening. By speaking aloud, you bring things from the unseen world into the seen world. Furthermore, there is research to show that by speaking things aloud, you hold yourself more accountable to achieving them.

Implementing Your Political Vision

Now that you have articulated your political vision, it's time to get clear on the action steps that will support the implementation of your vision. It's not as hard as you may think. I'm going to ask you a few questions to help you brainstorm so you get some concrete actions into place.

Pull out your Voice Journal and write for one minute, answering each question stream-of-consciousness style, per usual.

1. I know it might seem like a big leap now, but if you could imagine taking the first step to implement your political vision, what would it be?

2. What is one action step that you could encourage others to do to start implementing your political vision?

3. What is one action step that lawmakers and public policy officeholders could do to start implementing your political vision?

(Make sure to write down your responses to all of these questions. We will be using your responses later in the book for some leadership work.)

Gender-Balanced Leadership in Our Government

Although I am a proponent of creating change independent of the patriarchal system as I believe we need to build new feminine pathways for change, I do believe that entering the current system with our feminine ways is also an important piece of creating change.

I am an advocate for gender-balanced leadership in our government.

In the United States, at the current rate of progress for political representation, men will be the majority of political officeholders for the next 500 years.

That's pretty astounding, isn't it?

Currently, women in the United States represent only 19 percent of the voices in Congress, are only 10 percent of governors, and, in the nation's largest cities, only 13 percent of the mayors. (Women of color represent only 4 percent of the numbers in Congress, 4 percent of governors, 5 percent of state legislatures, and 2 percent of the mayors.)

As women are 51 percent of the population, our representation in our government is nowhere near a reflection of the reality of our presence in the United States of America.

This matters, and it matters a lot. It means that our political vision is not being heard in the halls of power and tables of leadership, and therefore not sufficiently part of public policy and the birthing of our laws.

According to a study by the Center of American Women and Politics titled, *The Impact of Women in Public Office*, women legislators bring different priorities to public office, including an emphasis on women's rights policies and legislation.

This seems logical, because a person's life experiences

characterize their approach to how they view and address issues that are brought to the tables in congress, city council and town hall, as well as how they speak about and address issues in the workplace, in the community and in the home.

There is no doubt that women and men experience life differently when it comes to issues of violence against women, sexual harassment, poverty, the wage gap, childcare policy, family and medical leave, healthcare, rights to our body, access to education, access to leadership positions, caring for the elderly, and a host of other issues.

Research from the Center for American Women and Politics revealed that with the increasing number of women in public office, there has been more attention paid to women's rights legislation and public policies related to women's traditional roles as caregiver in the family and society (i.e., children, childcare, healthcare, education, environment, housing and the elderly). The same policies that male legislators often ignored or diminished.

In the study, *The Impact of Women in Public Office*, a discussion group of female legislators reported saying to male legislators, "You know, these are your children, they are your mothers, your wives. If you are not going to take care of them, we are going to take care of them."

But are Democratic and Republican women on the same page when it comes to women's rights legislation and public policy affecting children and families?

While some may think that gender is not necessarily a determining factor in how women in office vote and approach issues, and that party affiliation has a stronger hold, this is actually not the case.

It turns out that Democratic and Republican women in office agree more on issues than not. This goes for citizens too.

A bipartisan survey by Lake Research Partners and

WomanTrend in 2012 found that regardless of political affiliation, 80 percent of women agreed on 80 percent of the issues.

The survey, *What Women Want 2012*, commissioned by the YWCA, was intended to bring to the attention of national and state leaders issues that are vitally important to women and their families. Researchers found that women agreed upon wanting Congress to take action on a range of economic and civil rights issues, including the Violence Against Women Act, equal pay, affordable healthcare, Social Security and Medicare. They also tended to support efforts to build consensus, solve problems and bring private and public interests together.

Pretty interesting, isn't it?

Marianne Williamson and Sister Giant

It might be that you've never considered running for political office. Or maybe you've thought about it, but decided it was out of your reach. I'd like to present an outlook, and a story of a life change, that may change your mind.

A couple of years ago Marianne Williamson came to speak at one of my women's groups in Los Angeles. For those of you not familiar with Marianne, she is a renowned spiritual teacher and *New York Times* bestselling author many times over. She didn't come that evening, however, to give us a spiritual teaching. She came to talk to us about politics.

That evening Marianne shared her plans for an event that she believed would change the course of American politics. It was called Sister Giant. Maybe some of you attended Sister Giant or have heard about it?

The intention of Sister Giant was to awaken and empower American women, on a personal growth path, to have a voice in politics.

"The entire political system is contrary to everything a feminine heart stands for," said Marianne. "It lacks tenderness. It lacks poetry. It doesn't nurture. It doesn't love. And without those things, a woman's soul is bereft."

Marianne's viewpoint was that women and men on a spiritual path – a path of personal growth, recovery, or even yoga – are the last people who should be sitting out the great social and political contests of our day. As she put it, "They're adepts at change; they know that the mechanics of the heart and mind are the drivers of true transformation."

Like Marianne Williamson, I believe that as women on a personal growth path, we need to start using our voices in the political arena. We need to start *leading* the conversations, instead of just following them. Or in some cases, running away from them.

***

The following year, Marianne announced her run for the United States House of Representatives in California District 33, representing Los Angeles area cities such as Santa Monica, Venice, Malibu, West Hollywood and Beverly Hills. This is my district.

While a lifelong Democrat, Marianne ran the race as an Independent. She wanted to make the statement that she is not beholden to either party and can make independent choices. "I believe that a wave of independent candidates, all committed to a huge course-correction, is necessary to turn our ship around. I feel my campaign, and most importantly my win, can help inspire such a movement," said Marianne in her campaign announcement speech in Los Angeles.

Marianne believed, as do I, that money has too strong an influence over politics. She often talked about the need to return American democracy to a government of the people, by the people, and for the people, instead of the current government "of a few of the people, by a few of the people, for a few of the people."

She was on a mission to create a new chapter in American history where our democratic principles of life, liberty and freedom were restored and the voices of citizens mattered again.

Marianne acknowledged that what she had to say would upset the current mode of operation, and that during the campaign, she may be mocked and minimized. But she insisted that despite this, she would continue to speak the truth of her heart.

And she did.

***

One of the many things Marianne brought to the tables of media, government and everyday citizens during her campaign was the need to create a constitutional amendment to overturn *Citizens United*, a 2010 court case that gave wealthy, secret donors unlimited power to manipulate American elections. In short, it legalized large-scale influence buying, ensuring that we would never know exactly who was purchasing certain politicians.

The law currently allows corporations to give unlimited amounts of money to political campaigns, and is considered a root culprit of the undue influence of money in politics.

She also gave people who hadn't participated in a

congressional campaign before – particularly those who had felt sidelined or cynical about the political process – the inspiration to exercise their own citizenship by paying attention, getting out to vote, and joining a campaign for change.

She encouraged women to re-envision their political possibilities and activated women who had never considered themselves political to get involved and interested in the political conversation.

While Marianne did not win her Congressional race (state senator Ted Lieu won the seat), by sharing her voice and her viewpoint, she reanimated the vision of Charlotta Spears Bass, a civil rights activist and the first black woman to run for vice president. In 1952, her campaign slogan was, "Win or lose, we win by raising the issues."

Sometimes that's exactly what it takes.

Like Marianne Williamson, I believe that as women on a personal growth path, we need to start using our voices in the political arena. Instead of just following the conversations, we need to be *leading* them.

Try this:

FEMININE LEADERSHIP PRACTICE

Step into your sacred space and set your timer for 2 minutes.

Heart Meditation. Your heart is the energy center that integrates your spiritual connection with your physical reality. It not only is a spectacular guidance system, but it generates the power you need to make political change. It's where your passion lies. Set your timer for 2 minutes for this practice.

- Sit comfortably in your sacred space in your meditation position.
- Inhale and exhale through your nose.
- Bring your hands to your heart.
- Allow your head to tilt downward to soften your thoughts.
- Inhale through your nose and into your heart space.
- Feel your heart expand.
- Exhale through your nose.
- Feel your heart relax.
- Repeat.
- Notice the rhythm of your heartbeat.
- Notice the feeling state of your heart.
- Keep breathing.
- Sit in silence and allow your breath to flow in and out.
- After 2 minutes when your timer sounds, finish your meditation with this mantra: "I am love. I am beauty. I am peace. I am grace."

FIND YOUR VOICE INTERVIEW

Take out your journal and a pen. Set a timer for 1 minute for each question. Answer each question in a stream-of-consciousness way. Do not edit yourself. Keep your pen to paper the whole time. Save your answers. We will be using your responses for some upcoming leadership work.

1. What did you discover in this chapter about your political vision?

2. In your wildest imagination, how do you see yourself implementing this political vision?

3. Who are the people you could partner with or build relationships with to quicken the manifestation of your political vision?

CHAPTER 5
Using Your Voice for Social Justice

"You have to give to the world the thing that you want the most, in order to fix the broken parts inside you."

– Eve Ensler

My first deep dive into social justice came about when I was in my mid-20s. I had recently returned from a six-month stay in India, where I was studying yoga and Tibetan Buddhism, teaching English to Tibetan monks living in exile, and leading a yoga class for Tibetan teenage girls who had been orphaned due to the political situation in Tibet.

During this time, I had fallen in love with Tibetans and Tibetan culture. I had also fallen into despair about the oppression of their religion and culture by the Chinese government and their exile from their own country.

When it was time for me to leave India, I knew that I could not leave the Tibetans behind. They were a part of me now. Their stories of imprisonment, beatings, and torture just for wanting to preserve their culture forever embedded into my heart and consciousness. I would not stay silent about what I had learned from them and about them. I would not stay silent because I knew so many of them were being silenced.

I had a voice to tell their story, and I was going to use it.

When I got to London, where I was going to be living with my American boyfriend who had a job there, I looked up a Tibetan organization I had learned about during my travels, The Free Tibet Campaign.

I called them up and told them that I wanted to work for them. I told them that I would do anything they needed, no matter if the job were big or small. "I just spent the last six months with Tibetans living in exile in India, and I can't *not* work for them," I said.

The Free Tibet Campaign invited me in for an interview. I started working with them the next day.

My first few weeks were spent opening and answering mail from supporters and donors. My next assignment was escorting an elderly Tibetan woman living in exile in India to three European embassies in London. My task was to help her get visas to visit officials in those countries to tell them the story of her son's unjust imprisonment by the Chinese.

Her son was a Fulbright scholar and student of ethnomusicology in America at Middlebury College. He went to Tibet in 1995 to make a film about the musical traditions of Tibet in an effort to preserve the history and oral tradition of this rich culture. While there, the Chinese officials accused him of being a spy, charged him with "espionage and counter-revolutionary activities," and threw him in prison, without trial, for an 18-year sentence. His mother was now looking for international support to demand the Chinese government free her son.

From there, I became a contributing writer to the *Free Tibet Magazine*, telling stories like this to others around the world so that the rest of the world knew about the Chinese human rights abuses and their oppression of Tibetans.

Later on, I was named editor of the magazine, where I curated stories from Tibetans as well as foreign internationals working for the Tibetan cause.

Fortunately, several years after I escorted the Tibetan mother, Sonam Dekyi, around to the European embassies, her efforts were successful and her son, Ngawang Choephel, was released, serving just seven years of the 18-year sentence.

In retrospect I see how my passion for the Tibetan cause was not only fueled by my love of the people I had met and my deep respect for their culture, but also my ability to relate to the pain of being silenced. In Eve Ensler's words, "You have to give to the world the thing that you want the most, in order to fix the broken parts inside you."

So what does this look like for you?

***

While you may have a big calling or vision, you don't have to accomplish it all in one swoop. Standing firm in your values and beliefs and using your voice to challenge the status quo is a very powerful organizing force. From there, you can take it step by step.

While your daily to-do lists are important and you need to take action to get things done, truly one of the most powerful ways to bring about social justice and cultural change is to simply *stand* for what you believe in and use your voice to let others know what's cooking inside of you.

Think about Rosa Parks, who refused to give up her seat on a bus to a white man in Montgomery, Alabama, in 1955. Her belief that she should have exactly the same rights as any other human being and her conviction to stand strong in this is what began the modern civil rights movement.

Think about Gloria Steinem who, after covering an abortion hearing as a journalist, began to question why abortion was illegal and why our reproductive lives weren't under our control. She was moved to action after hearing the testimony of women forced into the criminal underground as they sought abortions. She started to specifically cover the women-run movement against sexism (which was not getting nearly the serious attention it should have), and to write, speak out and organize around women's reproductive rights.

Gloria Steinem's perspective helped to bridge the divided groups of the movement and spurred the growth of the modern-day women's movement, second-wave feminism.

Think about Malala Yousafzai from Pakistan, who as a young girl refused to be silenced by the Taliban, who had banned girls from attending school. Malala used her voice as a blogger, then later as a speaker and media interviewee, speaking out for her right, and every girls' right, to an education.

At age 15, Malala was targeted by the Taliban and shot in the head at point-blank range while riding the bus home from school. Thank goodness she survived. Today, Malala travels the world championing universal access to education. She was awarded the Nobel Peace Prize in 2014 for her struggle against the suppression of children and for the right of all children to an education. Malala is the youngest person ever and the only person from Pakistan ever to receive the Nobel Peace Prize.

Think about Aung San Suu Kyi from Myanmar (Burma) who has spent most of the last two decades in detention for her efforts to bring democracy to her military-ruled country. In 1988, Aung San Suu Kyi was in England, studying at Oxford and caring for her two children. When she returned to her homeland to care for her critically-ill mother, she stepped into a land in the midst of major political upheaval. Myanmar's military government had one of the worst human rights records in the world, and in 1988, the streets swarmed with protesters. After seeing the demonstrations and hearing the cries of her countrywomen and men calling for democratic reform, Aung San Suu Kyi knew she couldn't remain indifferent to what was going on.

Aung San Suu Kyi stayed in Myanmar and became the leader of the revolt against then-dictator General Ne Win, organizing rallies and traveling around the country, calling for peaceful democratic reform and free elections. The demonstrations, however, were brutally suppressed by the army, who seized power in a coup. Soon after, Aung San Suu Kyi was put under house arrest.

Although she has spent most of the last two decades in detention for her efforts to bring democracy to her country, Aung San Suu Kyi is currently the party chairwoman of the National League for Democracy in Myanmar and has become an international symbol of peaceful resistance and leadership in the face of oppression.

Think about Leymah Gbowee in Liberia, who led a sisterhood of brave, visionary women in a peace movement to end the brutal civil war in her country. A mother of six children in despair over the brutality in her country, Leymah helped organize and then led a coalition of Christian and Muslim women who sat in public protest, confronting Liberia's ruthless president and rebel warlords, and even held a sex strike, refusing to have sex with their husbands until the men mobilized for peace.

Through Leymah's voice, conviction and leadership, the women's peace movement got the dictator leader, Charles

Taylor, removed and a woman president elected – the first woman president in Africa: President Ellen Johnson Sirleaf.

Think about Eve Ensler, who, as a young girl was a victim of incest and rape, and later as an adult woman turned her rage into positive action to reduce and heal sexual violence against women and girls.

As an off-off Broadway playwright in her early 30s, Eve found herself, as she puts it, "concerned about vaginas," and initiated a journey to interview women of all ages and races around the United States about their vaginas. She took the 200 interviews and turned them into poetry for theater, creating what is known today as *The Vagina Monologues.*

The Vagina Monologues became incredibly popular, spread nationally and internationally, and has been translated into 48 different languages and performed in more than 140 countries. Eve then grew it into the One Billion Rising Movement, activating women and men around the world to take a stand to end violence against women and urge legislators to enact laws and policies to bring perpetrators to justice.

All of these women stood, and are still standing, for what they felt deep inside was being asked of them. They used their voice. They stood their ground. And each one of them initiated a powerful social movement as a result of following their truth.

They had their to-do lists, I'm sure, and their days were filled with the small things that everyone had to get done. But they were able to hold on to, and manifest, a bigger vision.

I'd like to show you how you can do that, too. We're going to start with some simple exercises and build from there.

Activating Your Voice for Social Justice

Take out your Voice Journal and get ready to write.

Let's start with this:

What are the social injustices that you see happening around you (or that you are experiencing personally) that awaken your rage?

(i.e. inadequate domestic violence and rape laws, the wage gap, campus rape, hyper-sexualizing women in the media, gender-discrimination in the workplace, lack of sound family-leave and childcare policies, reproductive rights, racism, sexual assault, body shaming, victim blaming, corporate greed, undue influence of money in politics, . . .)

Take a moment to name them.

Now let's look internationally:

What are the social injustices that enrage you and that you wish you could put an end to?

(i.e., genital mutilation, bride burning, forced child marriage, sex trafficking, female infanticide, girls' lack of access to education, forced prostitution, women's lack of land rights, reproductive rights, . . .)

Now let's go here:

If you were to use your voice for a cause, what would it be?

If you know your answer right away, then write it down.

If you need some prompting, here are some causes to consider. Read through these and note what you feel most energized about:

- Ending the wage gap
- Eliminating all forms of violence against all women and girls
- De-stigmatizing domestic abuse and tightening laws against abusers
- Eliminating all harmful practices toward women and girls, such as child, early and forced marriage, and female genital mutilation
- Recognizing and valuing unpaid care and domestic work, and promoting shared responsibility within the household and the family
- Ensuring women's participation and leadership at all levels of decision-making in political, economic and public life
- Advancing childcare policies and childcare options for working parents
- Ensuring universal access to sexual and reproductive health and reproductive rights
- Undertaking reforms to give women equal rights to economic resources (land, property, financial services, inheritance and natural resources)
- Passage of the Equal Rights Amendment

What resonated for you? Where did you feel your passion?

If nothing resonated, but something else came to you, write that down now. We will build on this and come back to it in the chapters ahead, so be sure to keep your notes handy.

I want to share a story with you about a colleague of mine, Kamala Lopez, who took her jaw-dropping disbelief over a major social injustice and put her energy into action for positive social change.

Kamala, a filmmaker and actress, grew up like many of us, with the empowerment narrative telling her that she could be, do and have it all. She assumed, like many of us, that women and men had equal rights under the law. Why wouldn't we?

About six years ago, she had a wake up call that told her otherwise.

Kamala was in Washington, D.C., showing one of her films at the Smithsonian. In the lobby, she noticed a woman dressed up in a suffragist costume. The woman had been hired as a re-enactment actress to walk about the museum and educate people about the suffragist era. As a fellow actress with compassion for what some actresses who live outside of L.A. or New York need to do to earn money, Kamala welcomed the actress as she approached. "Who are you?" Kamala asked warmly.

"I'm Alice Paul back to haunt you because you haven't done anything to pass the Equal Rights Amendment."

Alice Paul, if you don't know who she is already, was a suffragist and the leader of the National Woman's Party who first authored the Equal Rights Amendment (ERA) and proposed it to Congress in 1923. This was three years after the passage of the 19th amendment guaranteeing women the right to vote.

Since 1923, activists have been trying to pass the ERA, which states, "Equality of rights under the law shall not be denied or abridged by the United States or by any State on account of sex."

Oh my God, we don't have equal rights?! Kamala thought. *This is completely ridiculous and unacceptable. What the hell is going on here?*

So what did Kamala do?

She went to find out why we this was the case. And you know what she found out?

That many women today, like her, believe that they have equal rights under the law and that their rights are already protected, and therefore no one is speaking up about it. In fact, according to the Equal Rights Coalition, 96 percent of Americans think the Equal Rights Amendment has passed.

In response, Kamala started the ERA Project to educate people about what is really going on, and to build a platform to change it. The project includes a feature-length documentary film, *Equal Means Equal*, and a website, eraeducationproject.com. Through both of these, Kamala is educating Americans on what the Equal Rights Amendment actually is, why we need it, and how to get the ERA passed. "235 years is kind of a long time to wait for equal rights," says Kamala.

***

At the time of writing this, Kamala is in the final stages of editing *Equal Means Equal*, which she raised money for through Kickstarter, and is already showing clips around the country. This year at the Oscars, Oscar-winner Patricia Arquette, a longtime friend of *Equal Means Equal*, gave a shout out to the film backstage during her media interviews. This has built significant buzz for the film and is attracting potential distributors. Kamala says when the film is released, it will be "an unprecedented cinematic wake-up call for America."

I believe it.

Kamala's story is an example of how one woman took her outrage over a social injustice and used her voice, talents and skills to turn it into positive social action. I invite you to add your own story to these tales of positive social action.

In the words of Eve Ensler, "An activist is someone who cannot help but fight for something. That person is not usually motivated by a need for power or money or fame, but in fact is driven slightly mad by some injustice, some cruelty, some unfairness, so much so that he or she is compelled by some internal moral engine to act to make it better."

So what will you stand for and how will you do it?

Make sure to do today's leadership practice and journal exercises to get the answers.

Try this:

FEMININE LEADERSHIP PRACTICE

Step into your sacred space. Set your timer for 2 minutes.

Chanting. Chanting is a practice that helps us connect our inner, intuitive voice with our outer, worldly voice. When practiced on a regular basis, it will help you become more confident in using your voice publicly in a way that is connected to your soul. Take 2 minutes for this feminine leadership practice.

- Sit comfortably in your sacred space in your meditation position.
- Allow your eyes to soften.
- Inhale and exhale through your nose a few times.
- After a deep inhale, allow the sound of OM ("ommmm") to release out of you on an exhale. OM is a sound that connects us to the universal nature of life.
- Chant OM three times.
- As you chant, feel the sound vibrate throughout the cells of your body.
- Feel the connection between your pelvic area, belly and throat.
- On your next round of breaths, instead of OM, chant MA ("maaaaaa"). MA is a sound to honor the Divine Feminine aspect of our nature.
- Chant MA three times.

- As you chant, feel the sound vibrate throughout the cells of your body. Allow this chant to be a celebration and deep honoring of your femininity and the feminine nature of life.
- Finish by bowing your head to your heart.
- Offer gratitude to both your inner voice and your outer voice.

FIND YOUR VOICE INTERVIEW

Take out your journal and a pen. Set a timer for 1 minute for each question. Answer each question in a stream-of-consciousness way. Do not edit yourself. Keep your pen to paper the whole time. Save your answers. We will be using your responses for some upcoming leadership work. Please note that you may have answered a variation of some of these questions earlier in the book. There's a purpose to this. Being asked the same question from a slightly different angle will help you to further own and integrate this language into your daily living.

1. What is one social injustice that you feel most emotionally charged by, and feel like if you had a platform, you would do something about it?

2. In looking at the social injustice that you are most irked (or outraged) by, what are the values and practices that you would like to put forth in its place?

3. What are the skills and talents that you have that you could put into action to address this social injustice?

CHAPTER 6
Owning Your Feminine Authority

"The worship of female deities appeared in every area around the world, presenting an image of woman that I had never before encountered."

– Merlin Stone

So many of us have been made to feel that something is wrong with us simply because we are female. We have been made to feel "less than," unimportant, or second-class. As women, we have doubted our self-worth, self-knowledge and self-authority, all in the name of patriarchy.

God the Father. Jesus, Son of God. Allah. Buddha. Brahma.

With a man "at the top" of every major world religion, is it any wonder women and girls feel less than worthy? Whether we consider ourselves religious or not, this male spiritual leadership holds immense power in our cultural consciousness.

I personally did not grow up in a religious household, but I most certainly absorbed the idea that "God the Father" was at the helm. As a young girl in school, every day I pledged allegiance to the flag of the United States of America, embedding into my consciousness the mantra: "One nation under God, indivisible, with liberty and justice for all." Ha!

At my brother's guitar recitals, I joined in the sing-alongs, cheerfully clapping and singing: "He's got the whole world in His hands. He's got the whole world in His hands. He's got the whole world in His hands . . ."

I often wonder, what if I grew up every day pledging my allegiance to one nation under Goddess, or Mother God? What if I instead were singing, "She's got the whole world in Her hands. She's got the whole world in Her hands . . ."

And what if boys grew up this way too?

If we, as individuals and as a culture, see "God" and refer to God only in male terms, being a man or being a boy becomes more "Godlike" or "Divine" than being a woman or girl. Maleness then becomes the standard by which we measure things, and the aspirations of humankind. We all want to be Divine, right?

What also happens with this orientation is that being a man or being masculine becomes synonymous with holding the ultimate authority, and having power to exercise that authority. Femininity, by default, takes on the quality of being "second-class," of lesser value, and, most definitely, of lesser authority.

When seen in this light, it becomes pretty obvious why we women are working so hard, yet still struggling to gain leadership status within our workplace, government, media, and very specifically, our religious communities (unless we are in a feminine-based community).

It also explains why we would have so much self-doubt around our qualifications and ability to be leaders. For instance, take what's going on in our careers. According to recent research, men are applying for jobs if they meet 60 percent or more of the qualifications, while women are tending to apply only if they meet 100 percent of the qualifications.

Pretty telling, isn't it?

Living in a paradigm where men and the masculine are seen as the rightful owners of authority, and women and the feminine are the underclass, it's no wonder that so many women second-guess themselves, their qualifications, and their voice in the world.

The image of a male God has been so deeply internalized by us that it exercises power over everything, including questioning our own feminine authority.

The Untold History of Female Power

In the ninth grade, when I was first learning about ancient civilizations, I was taught that men were the ones making history. They were the culture builders, they were the warriors, they were the lawmakers. Accordingly, I walked through much of my life with an unexamined assumption that men have always held power in the world.

But this is simply not true.

There is an untold history of female power where women held religious, economic and political leadership. Did you know that archeologists and scholars have found that Goddess culture existed for 30,000 years before the patriarchy?

Yes, that's right. Artifacts related to the religion of the Goddess and the worship of female deities appeared in every area of the world, including the Middle East, Eastern, Western and Northern Europe, the Mediterranean, Africa, Egypt, Southeast Asia, India, Australia, China and Russia.

Numerous sculptures of female figurines made of stone, bone, clay and ivory, cave paintings and carvings, pottery, temple sites and ritual items all related to the Goddess have been found, spanning a time period of 30,000 years.

Pretty amazing, right?

According to British historian Bettany Hughes, if you look at all the human figurines that were made from 40,000 B.C. to 1000 B.C., you will find that 92 percent of those are of the female form.

What a presence we had!

The Goddess was celebrated as the supreme deity, and was known by countless names, depending on the culture – Isis, Lilith, Ashtoreth, Ishtar, Queen of Heaven, the Great Goddess, Inanna, Hathor, Aphrodite, Tara, Kali, Brigid, Astarte, and more. She was worshipped in many aspects and was seen as the creative force, giver of life, producer of food, protector, healer, wisdom teacher, lover and sensual beauty.

Due to women's power to give birth, women were associated with the Goddess, the giver of life, and were given respect accordingly. This was seen in the female-centered way of life in the Goddess-worshiping cultures, where women held prominent positions in these societies.

As art historian Merlin Stone describes in her book, *When God Was a Woman*, women bought and sold property, traded in the marketplace, controlled the food supply, and inherited title and land from their mothers. She describes how these Goddess-worshipping societies were matrilineal, with names, titles, possessions and territorial rights passing through the female line.

According to mythologist Robert Graves, in these early societies, the concept of fatherhood had not yet been introduced into religious thought.

One of the leading pioneers to uncover the story and bring together a comprehensive understanding of the Goddess was Lithuanian archeologist and UCLA archeology professor, Marija Gimbutas.

Marija spent 30 years studying the patterns, symbols and objects of the Goddess in an area she named Old Europe. She wrote more than 20 books on the topic, including *The Civilization of the Goddess* and *The Language of the Goddess*.

In her books, Marija describes a Goddess-oriented civilization that lived in peace, in harmony with nature, with a striking absence of images of warfare and male domination, and with a high degree of economic, social and sexual equality.

The Decline of the Goddess

So what happened to the Goddess and the feminine-based culture?

It all started to go downhill over a two-thousand-year period, beginning around 4500 B.C., when waves of northern people, generally known as Indo-Europeans, invaded the Goddess-worshipping areas of the Near East, bringing with them their own religion – the worship of a young warrior god and/or a supreme father god.

As the invaders gained more territories, they grew more and more powerful and eventually the male god replaced the female Goddess in every culture. The warrior rose in social power, and as this happened, the social power of women as a group declined.

At this time, worship of the Goddess was outlawed, and some say that the patriarchal images, customs and laws in the male religious cultures were developed in direct reaction to Goddess worship, making sure to position women as the "underclass."

Why We Don't Know Her Story

It can feel infuriating to have this important part of our human story omitted from our history books and history classes. I have often wondered how all of our lives might be different if every girl and boy learned about the 30,000-year history of the Goddess that existed before the onset of patriarchal religion and culture.

I'm not pretending that a history lesson about the Goddess in middle school would have a life-altering impact on every kid in the classroom, but I imagine it would change their frame of reference about who held power in the world, and certainly give girls a sense of their rightful place as leaders. Boys as well might not be so self-assuming about their superior position in the world. This would, I believe, lead to a more open field for leadership.

One key factor to why we don't learn about the ancient Goddess religion in history class is the overwhelming prevalence of male scholars, historians and theologians who were raised in societies that embraced the male-oriented religions. They wrote our history books. They teach history and religion.

Of the few women who worked in these disciplines, they were also raised in societies that embraced the male-oriented religions, and may not have even thought to challenge these ideas, or were well aware that challenging the male powers would bring harm to them. (Think: witch burnings and other forms of persecution.)

Religious narratives are written by the victors: the invaders, often the oppressors, certainly those in power. Those on top had an interest in consolidating their power in order to stay on top, and so they made sure their religious narratives legitimized the patriarchal warrior culture and diminished the Goddess.

One clear example of this is the story of Adam and Eve.

For many of us, we heard the story of Adam and Eve at a very young age. Whether we regarded the story as myth or truly the creation story, it permeates our culture and has made its way into our unconscious.

A quick review: Woman (Eve) was created out of man (Adam). She was then told by an Almighty man (God) not to pick a forbidden fruit (apple). She picked it (disobedience) – gave it to Adam (unsuspecting innocence) – and from then on was said to have committed the first sin. It was that simple picking, which perhaps was due to pioneering curiosity, that is said to have led to the fall of humanity from paradise and the introduction of evil into the world.

Assuming Eve as the archetype of woman, woman here is portrayed as undisciplined, disobedient, and a sinner. Looking at it this way, it's no wonder that women have an underlying sense of blame, shame and, in many cases, a fear of questioning male authority.

The story of Eve also conveys that female will and female nakedness must be controlled and punished by a male authority. This part of our spiritual and cultural heritage seems an obvious contributor to women's inferiority complex.

In contrast, Goddess images show females as powerful and almighty. They show us the goodness of the female body and female power.

Feminine Spiritual Role Models

With all this in mind, I think it's important to look at how we would feel if our spiritual leader were depicted as a woman and referred to as a "She." Would we feel any different? Would we feel our center of authority? Would we inhabit more space? Would we walk with confidence and assume authority simply from being a woman?

What is your reaction to even considering this?

Since the decline of the Goddess religion, women have lacked spiritual role models and systems that speak to our needs and experiences. Instead, we have been taught to identify with masculine values as our spiritual ideals. This largely includes denying our bodies and the sacred nature of our sexuality, a great source of our power.

I believe that it's the disconnection from our sacred self – our feminine self – our Goddess within – that has disconnected us from our own value and ability to own our feminine authority.

Why the Goddess Is Important to Women's Leadership

Not enough women, myself included, have honored our feminine world view. We have underestimated the importance and significance of our values, our belief systems and our visions for the future.

Learning about the Goddess and the Divine Feminine can change this for us. Knowing about *herstory* gives us a new vantage point, one that legitimizes female power and honors feminine authority. In other words, knowledge of this part of our human story stirs us to question our culture's ingrained view that all legitimate power is male.

Many people depend on religion as their moral compass; they feel they would be lost without the guidance of a god. If that guidance is solely being provided by a male god, where does that leave women? Viewed in that primal way, there can be no doubt that excluding women from spiritual leadership diminishes their status in society, and undercuts their authority.

As we learn about the ancient Goddess religion and cultures, we get to re-evaluate the information that has come to us through patriarchal sources. We start to wake up to the fact that most everything written about us is *without* us. We also begin to understand that we do not have to live as we do today. Our values, beliefs and vision for the future do matter. And when put into practice, can make the world a different place.

The Goddess helps us heal the deep wound in us that tells us we are unworthy. Knowledge of Her helps us call into question our current social system, and gives us a new framework for understanding our experience. It also provokes a reconsideration of the roles of women in society. The Goddess provides a very different image of womanhood than that which is offered by the male-oriented religions of today.

When you learn about our human story in all its richness, with its feminine side intact, it will orient you in an entirely new way. This knowledge, once obtained, will make you call into question your long-held views about power and authority and shatter long-standing cultural attitudes about women (that includes yourself).

Imagine what effect learning about the Goddess could have on a girl's self-esteem as she develops into a young woman.

As we learn about Her Story, it awakens us to challenge some basic assumptions about leadership, and that's exactly what we need to do as trailblazing feminine leaders of the 21st century.

Suggested Further Reading

If you want to go deeper into the study of feminine history, here are some of my favorite books.

- *When God Was a Woman*, by Merlin Stone
- *The Chalice and the Blade*, by Rianne Eisler
- *The Politics of Women's Spirituality*, edited by Charlene Spretnak
- *Language of the Goddess*, by Marija Gimbutas
- *The Living Goddesses*, by Marija Gimbutas
- *Shakti Woman*, by Vicki Noble
- *The Great Cosmic Mother: Rediscovering the Religion of the Earth*, by Monica Sjoo & Barbara Mor
- *Rebirth of the Goddess*, by Carol Christ
- *The Spiral Dance*, by Starhawk

When a Woman Learns About the Goddess

She discovers that she doesn't need permission from male authority to rise in her leadership.

She IS leadership.

When a woman learns about the Goddess . . .

She is inspired to create music, art, poetry, theater and dance to express and manifest the grandness of her vision.

When a woman learns about the Goddess . . .

She sees the goodness of her female body and begins to honor it as sacred.

When a woman learns about the Goddess . . .

She begins to see herself as powerful and almighty as she is awakened to herself as Divine Creatix.

When a woman learns about the Goddess . . .

She begins to accept and respect her own authority, as she discovers her connection to a powerful lineage of female spiritual, economic, social and political leadership.

When a woman learns about the Goddess . . .

She begins to heal the deep wound within her that tells her she is unworthy.

When a woman learns about the Goddess . . .

She begins to change the way she views and values herself.

When a woman learns about the Goddess . . .

She begins to see that she needs no one's permission.

She needs no gatekeeper to let her in.

She is in.

She IS.

Try this:

FEMININE LEADERSHIP PRACTICE

Step into your sacred space. Set your timer for 3 minutes.

Divine Mother Movement. As women, we hold wisdom in our body that has been passed down through centuries and millennia of feminine lineage, connected to the source of creation – the womb of the Goddess. Sometimes accessing this wisdom can only happen in very subtle ways, with a deep sense of listening. Today's practice will help you cultivate this skill and tool of deep listening. Allow yourself 3 minutes for this feminine leadership practice.

- Come into your sacred space and stand with your feet hips-distance apart.
- Allow your eyes to soften.
- Inhale and exhale through your nose a few times.
- After a deep inhale, allow the sound of MA to release out of you on an exhale. (You did this practice in the last chapter, MA is a sound to honor the Divine Feminine.)
- Chant MA three times.
- As you chant, feel the sound vibrate throughout the cells of your body.
- Feel the connection between your womb and your throat.
- On your next round of breaths, allow yourself to explore different tones of MA. See how your body responds with different tonality.

- Next, invite your body to move gently and subtly as you continue to chant your MAs.
- As you move and chant, feel the sound vibrate throughout the cells of your body. Allow your subtle movements and sounding to nourish the feminine wisdom and intelligence that you carry within you.
- After about a minute, allow your voice to get quiet, and invite your body into stillness.
- Breathe.
- Listen deeply to the internal intelligence of your body. How does She want to move?
- Invite your body's internal intelligence to guide you. Feel what's happening in your body. Where is energy flowing? Invite Her – your body's feminine intelligence – to move you. (As opposed to you moving Her.)
- Breathe.
- Keep listening deeply to how your body wants to move, without you directing Her. Surrender to this intelligence. The movements may be very subtle, or may come in the form of rushing energy, or something entirely different. See how She – the Goddess – wants to move through you.
- Finish by bringing one hand to your heart and the other hand to your womb area. Rest there for a few moments.
- Bow your head to your heart and your womb, honoring your body's natural feminine intelligence and your connection to the Divine Feminine within you.

FIND YOUR VOICE INTERVIEW

Take out your journal and a pen. Set a timer for 1 minute for each question. Answer each question in a stream-of-consciousness way. Do not edit yourself. Keep your pen to paper the whole time and write from your intuitive self. Save your answers. We will be using your responses for some upcoming leadership work.

1. On what topics and issues do you feel you have authority because of your personal experience, but have been not giving yourself enough credit for?

2. What are the reasons you feel you deny yourself your feminine authority?

3. If you gave yourself permission to use your authority, where would you be and what would you be doing?

CHAPTER 7
Breaking Through Visibility Fears

"And the day came when the risk to remain tight in a bud was more painful than the risk it took to blossom."

– Anais Nin

Many of the women who come to me for leadership coaching tell me that they want to have a bigger voice in the world. They want to have more influence, and build something that matters; yet at the same time, they have fears around visibility.

Some of them are able to clearly identify these fears – such as the fear of taking up "too much" of the spotlight, being called a "show-off," sounding "stupid," being accused of being "wrong," or being challenged on their ideas and values.

Then there are others who aren't quite able to put their finger on why they feel so scared. They tell me that they have made strides in their leadership, but for some reason they can't go all the way. They keep getting tripped up. They come forward. Then they go back. They come forward. Then they go back. Forward. Back. Forward. Back. Like a little turtle going into her shell for safety and retreat.

I notice when these women come to me, they have a lot of confusion around what's going on, and also massive self-judgment.

Why do I keep getting stuck? What is wrong with me? Why is this taking me so long? Why am I so scared to become visible and be that feminine leader I know I am meant to be?

I get it. I've been there. I know how painful it is.

Since my work revolves around the Goddess and one of my main messages is about how feminine spirituality is a missing link to advancing more women in leadership, I have had huge fears around sounding like a loony and being taken to the "crazy house" when I talk about this.

A big fear of mine for a long time was that if I was challenged, would I be able to back up my argument with facts? I was paralyzed by this fear. Whenever I pictured myself speaking about this message in public, I envisioned I would freeze in silence, and then burn red with embarrassment because I couldn't present the cold, hard facts in a "logical" way.

I realized later that this was because a lot of what I knew and wanted to speak about came from deep within my soul, so this could not always be backed up by cold, hard facts.

As I entered into more and more women's circles, I learned that my experience was common among women. What many of us know comes from deep inside, connected to a feminine lineage that has long been silenced. For this reason, the "facts" aren't always readily available to us, and even if they are, what we have to say usually is something that challenges the status quo.

In my case, because of this, I was much more comfortable learning from others and being the "student" rather than stepping into my dharma as a leader and teacher.

But eventually this comfort grew into discomfort. I was so uncomfortable with keeping myself small; keeping my voice hidden; keeping my truths and my power inside. I knew I was meant for bigger things – bigger stages, bigger platforms, bigger venues. But I was not allowing myself all of this. I was terrified to stand up in front of people and voice my truth – even though I knew this was my destiny.

Does this sound familiar to you? Have you had an experience like this?

One of my favorite quotes is from author and diarist Anaïs Nin. She said: "And the day came when the risk to remain tight in a bud was more painful than the risk it took to blossom." I first learned of this quote in college, and it has been with me ever since. It has given me the strength and the foresight to see that taking the risk to blossom is worth it.

There is so much trauma and wounding around women's voices, especially when it comes to speaking about things that challenge the status quo. We have been burned at the stake (yes, those witch burnings are still alive in our consciousness), tortured, murdered, raped, and dismissed as "hysterical" for speaking our truth and coming forward with our belief systems. This all is in our collective consciousness, and is a real doozy that holds us back.

Whether we are conscious of it or not, it's very real.

Last year I went through a major journey with this collective memory. As I was developing a coaching program called the Goddess Leadership Program, I was stepping up my leadership in a bigger way and becoming more and more visible. Through this program, I was standing for the recognition and reverence of the Goddess as a significant missing link to women's leadership in the 21st century, a sincere challenge to the status quo of patriarchal culture and religion.

(It's important to point out here that over eight million women were burned at the stake in medieval Europe in an effort to wipe out the remains of pre-Christian religion that honored women.)

Since what I was standing for is not part of our mainstream conversation, I was experiencing some major visibility challenges – some of which were taking me down the road of our feminine collective memory. Luckily, I was receiving some insights too. Big shout out here to my cranio-sacral therapist, Maura Moynihan, who held space for me with her enormous loving soul to traverse this territory so I could name it, heal it and move forward.

From this experience, I learned that, as women, we need to bring this conversation of our collective memory that holds so many of us back – out of the closet and into our circles. Talk about it with friends. Talk about it with our mentors and coaches. Talk about it with our sisters. Write about it. Speak about it. Let it breathe and release.

We also need to offer ourselves some compassion around this. This is deep stuff. If you catch yourself beating yourself up about not being where you think you are supposed to be or berate yourself by telling yourself a story that you don't have the capacity to be in leadership, I invite you to take a deep breath and send yourself some love instead. Becoming more visible as a feminine leader is a vulnerable place to be, and you deserve love for your courage, not scorn.

***

To set the stage for your practice today, I want to share with you some thoughts from one of my clients. When she was struggling with using her voice and becoming visible in alignment with her soul's purpose, I asked her to write a short essay about what happens when a woman is not self-expressed. Here is what she wrote . . .

WHAT HAPPENS WHEN A WOMAN IS NOT SELF-EXPRESSED?

She dies on the vine. She shrivels. She becomes hard. As her vitality shrinks, the shell surrounding her heart becomes a carapace. She becomes unrecognizable to herself until she forgets who she ever was. She can no longer hear the call of her heart or her soul; perhaps they've stopped speaking to her altogether, feeling pointless. She has a persistent feeling of discontent. She feels false, as if she daily dons an ill-fitting suit or a suffocating, heavy costume. It weighs her down, it muffles her, it disguises her to the world and from herself. Yet, there's something that's always wanting to come out. She stops participating. Her world gets small, insular. She doesn't remember the last time she laughed or had a real hug or was touched. She's angry, so very angry. She figures, "Why bother?" and the fear of being disappointed leads to more disappointment. She wants to rent a soundproof room and YELL and get it out until there's nothing left. As she gets older, she fears she will die having made one colossal mess of it and wasted her life and time wishing, yearning, unfulfilled, and sad.

– Connie V.

Try this:

FEMININE LEADERSHIP PRACTICE

Step into your sacred space and set your timer for 2 minutes.

Visualize the Transformation. I invite you to take a few moments to visualize the change that will happen in people's lives when you come forward as a leader with your message, whether it be through business, artistry, political leadership, the healing arts, advocacy, motherhood, etc. Allow yourself not only to see, but *feel* in this exercise. It's important to understand the transformation you are creating in people's lives in order to keep yourself inspired to move through whatever doubts, fears and insecurities come up along the way (and they will) as you step out bigger and more visibility as a leader. Take 2 minutes for this practice.

- Sit comfortably in your sacred space in your meditation position.
- Close your eyes.
- Inhale and exhale through your nose a few times.
- Begin to tune in to the people your leadership and greater visibility will benefit.
- See these people. Feel these people. Hear these people. Let your heart open and connect eye-to-eye with these people.
- Deliver your message to these people.

- Notice their response. What is happening in their body? What is happening in their eyes? What is happening in their essence?
- Talk with these people. Engage. Interact.
- What are you noticing?
- How were they before you delivered your message? How are they now? Acknowledge the transformation.
- Finish by bringing your hands to your heart and bowing your head to your heart.
- Vow that you will not let these people down.
- Breathe.
- Slowly open your eyes.

FIND YOUR VOICE INTERVIEW

Take out your journal and a pen. Set a timer for 1 minute for each question. Answer each question in a stream-of-consciousness way. Do not edit yourself. Keep your pen to paper the whole time. Save your answers. We will be using your responses for some upcoming leadership work.

1. What do you feel you are most afraid of when it comes to becoming more visible?

2. What do you feel is at stake if you continue to play small and/or hide from the spotlight?

3. What is your biggest vision for yourself? (Describe yourself in your most public persona. Include everything here.)

CHAPTER 8
Unleashing Your Creative Expression

"Inevitably, perhaps because experiences of the sacred are so deep and deeply personal, creative acts of expression are expressions of awakening that begin with trusting our own feelings and perceptions, of realizing it is up to us to be real and act on the premise that what matters to us really matters."

– Jean Shinoba Bolen

Art is an integral part of a cultural system, and has a significant influence on its political system and ideology. Like most women, though, you were probably not taught to look at your feminine artistry and creative expression as powerful forces for social and political change. In fact, you may have even been belittled or mocked for your effusive creative expressions as a young girl, been taught not to trust your creative impulses, or had your creativity "educated" out of you.

When you feel the creative spark now, you may question it, silence it, or even belittle it yourself. This is a definite setback for your leadership.

As women, we express our wisdom not only through speech and logic, but through every form of creative expression, such as dance, movement, song, chant, music, spoken word, art, poetry, storytelling, ritual, creative writing, videos, filmmaking, and so much more. In other words, we transmit and disseminate our wisdom through our feminine artistry.

Art is how we give birth to feminine consciousness on the planet. Art is how we express ourselves from the deepest levels of our soul. Art is how we liberate our voices and our bodies from patriarchal-induced silencing and shaming. Art is an invitation for us to thrive.

Think about folk, pop and jazz singers who changed the social stream toward peace, humanity and civil rights, like Joan Baez, Joni Mitchell and Nina Simone. Or writers who gave voice to women's oppression, like Simone De Beauvoir with *The Second Sex* and Betty Friedan with *The Feminine Mystique*, and inspired contemporary feminism.

Or novelists who instilled subtle feminist ideals to empower women to find their own unique paths, like Jane Austen and Charlotte Bronte. Or diarists who gave voice to feminine sensuality and desire, like Anaïs Nin, and liberated women in their sexual expression.

Think about feminist filmmakers who have highlighted societal problems that were being overlooked, like Jennifer Siebel Newsom did with *Miss Representation* when she called out mainstream media for their degrading portrayals of women and girls.

Or screenwriters like Callie Khouri who broke the Hollywood stereotype of women in passive roles and dependent on men by writing a story of empowered women making independent choices for themselves in the film "Thelma and Louise."

Poets like Maya Angelou have touched upon the universal truths of womanhood and have given voices to women everywhere with poems like "I Know Why the Caged Bird Sings," "Still I Rise" and "Phenomenal Woman."

Playwrights like Eve Ensler opened up a national, and later international, discussion of women's vaginas and female sexuality through *The Vagina Monologues*, later growing the passion for the topic into the One Billion Rising Movement, where women and men from around the world are rising to take a stand to end violence against women and girls. From these risings, laws and public policies are being implemented around the world to advance the protection of women and their bodies.

Did you ever consider that expressing yourself creatively in your true feminine nature is a very important political act?

***

As a young girl, one of my favorite things to do was sing and dance.

I loved to put on performances for my mom and my neighbors, get up on my "stage" (a large windowsill), and go all out singing "The Sun Will Come Out Tomorrow" from the Broadway play *Annie*. I had no problem belting at the top of my lungs with full emotional tilt.

Being the youngest of three children (I have two older brothers), and a member of a very strong male lineage, my effusive emotional and theatrical expression was not always met with support and cheer. Moreso, it was met with teasing and mockery.

So I learned to shut this part of myself down.

An initial chipping away of my authentic voice.

***

What I have come to realize through my work with clients over the years is that a woman's leadership is thwarted if she cannot creatively express herself, because it is her creative expression that is the doorway into her soul's purpose.

Take my client Connie for example, whose essay you read in the previous chapter. Connie came to me with the desire to, as she put it, "build something that matters." The problem was she had no idea what that something was. All she knew is that she felt pregnant with possibility and wanted to bring something into the world that had the power to transform individual lives, as well as the socio-political collective.

Connie enrolled in my VIP women's leadership program – Creating Your Feminine Legacy. We worked together for six months to figure this thing out.

During my early discussions with Connie, she shared with me that she felt her passions, emotional energy, talents and skills were all over the place, and that she was "flailing about." She was a construction litigation lawyer in New York City, and yet was passionate about animals and animal welfare, nature and earth justice, and was a talented, yet not fully self-expressed, singer and photographer.

She felt that her array of interests and passions were keeping her from finding her greater purpose. She wanted to take concrete forward action, on a regular basis, on one issue, but could not take that all-important first step.

"I have all these great ideas. I play with them like peas on a plate. But it's all scattered. They don't get traction," she told me.

As Connie and I worked together, we began to get curious about her passion and talent for photography, and set up some assignments to explore and exercise the muscles of this creative expression.

And what did Connie want to photograph? Animals.

When Connie showed me her photographs – one of an owl, another of a turtle, another of a dog, another of a horse – I was moved deeply. Connie had captured the soul of these animals through *their eyes*. It was clear that something very special was going on here between Connie and her photo subjects.

We continued to send Connie out on assignments to give her greater access to this form of expression. She enrolled in a photography class to sharpen her skills, and soon enough her photos were being featured in a SoHo gallery in New York.

Several weeks after this, Connie had a singing performance scheduled, something she had not done in many years. But during our time working together she had signed up for a singing class, which offered a performance as a culmination of the experience.

This performance was a breakthrough moment for Connie. It was here that she began to reclaim her authentic voice and clear the pathway for what was about to come next.

Through a morning practice, which we called *Sing, Groove, Move*, Connie began to dust off the cobwebs and connect to a former self she had long since abandoned. She started to "out" her inner artist that had been suffering in silence for a long time due to earlier unsupportive social conditioning.

It was around this time that I invited Connie to write the essay you read in the previous chapter, "What Happens When a Woman Is Not Self-Expressed?"

Like so many girls and young women who are not encouraged in their creative expression, Connie had been told at a young age that her skills in the performing arts were not "good enough," and that she should abort pursuing this path. A clear chipping away of her authentic voice.

As Connie continued her *Sing, Groove, Move* practice as well as her photography, her voice began to open up and strengthen, and so did her confidence and self-authority. This became the key to what happened next: Connie, for the first time, began to integrate her skills as a lawyer, photographer and performance artist, with her passion for animal rights.

Today Connie is a District Leader for the Humane Society of the United States, representing New York City, where she lobbies for animal rights and uses her photography to advance her cases and arguments. Furthermore, she's got a one-woman show in production, which is dedicated to raising funds and awareness for animal rights and welfare.

It may seem like an indirect pathway at first, but when Connie started to reawaken her expressive self, she unlocked the door to her truest expression as an activist. She was then able to leverage all her skills to realize her soul's purpose.

So would you like to look at some ways you can turn your feminine creativity into a force for social and political change?

Identify Your Creative Expression

Take out your journal and pen and get ready to do a stream-of-consciousness writing. Take 30 seconds for each question.

1. What did you love to do as a 7-, 8- or 9-year-old? Sing, dance, write, paint, play an instrument, create rituals . . .? How did you creatively express yourself? What came naturally to you? Write this down.

2. What is a form of creative expression you do where you feel "at one" with yourself?

3. Your creative expression may be at the forefront of your work in the world and may be your income earner, or it may be a channel for you to connect to your deeper purpose and empower your voice in the world. Or it may be both. How do you imagine your creative expression supports your political vision? Is it at the forefront, or is it a support channel?

Make a "Creative Expression" Date

Mark out 30 minutes in your calendar later this week to engage in one of your forms of creative expression. Whether it's singing, dancing, poetry, spoken word, painting, photography, drumming, or another form of your expression. Whatever it is, commit to this time as a sacred date with your feminine soul. Allow the art form to be a container for your feminine soul to be expressed.

Build a Daily or Weekly Practice

Once you've had your Creative Expression Date, I highly recommend building a creative expression practice (if you don't already have one), to continually unleash your wisdom through the practice. In working with my clients, I help them set up a practice that is extremely practical for them. Nothing overwhelming. With Connie, for example, we set up a weekly photo prompt to get her photographing on a regular basis, and a *Sing, Groove, Move* practice three days a week. That worked well for her.

What will your daily or weekly practice be?

Transforming Your Creativity into Activism

I know it can feel daunting to get out there with your creative expression. As I talked about in earlier chapters, when we step out further as a feminine leader, visibility issues creep in, especially if your message is flat out against the status quo.

This stuff is real and we can't try to brush it under the rug.

I believe that when we creatively express ourselves, the stories about us that are not true go away, and so do the injustices that those untruths support. Untruths such as: women are the weaker sex, are not as smart as men, are sexual objects, are not as qualified for leadership, are dependent on men for survival. These grow dim in the bright light of our honesty, and the courage generated by telling our own, more truthful, stories about ourselves.

When you express your creative truth as a woman, you not only liberate your own self, but you open up the door for other women to express their truth as well. And as this happens, we start shifting the tides of society. The ripple effect is set in motion and what's out there in the public consciousness changes.

This is feminine activism – an activism that stems from inspiration, creativity and embodiment, and has the potential to dramatically shift our socio-political conversation to one with a new feminine consciousness.

When you give yourself permission to reveal your deepest feminine soul expression, you naturally embody your feminine authority and power. This re-orientation and acceptance of your power inherently shifts the status quo, and *is* social and political change.

Try this:

FEMININE LEADERSHIP PRACTICE

Step into your sacred space and set your timer for 2 minutes.

Lion Mama. This practice is all about letting go of inhibition. It's time to let your inner fire spark great change in the world. The more you let loose in the privacy of your sacred space, the more trust you will create in yourself that you will be okay in public when you get more expressive and start to take up more space. Take 2 minutes for this feminine leadership practice.

- Sit comfortably in your sacred space in your meditation position.
- Soften your eyes.
- Inhale and exhale through your nose a few times.
- Transition to a position where you are sitting on your heels.
- Breathe in and breathe out.
- Take one big inhale, and on your exhale pounce forward with a BIG MAMA LION'S ROAR.
- Repeat this 10 times, allowing your roar to get BIGGER & BIGGER each time. Take up more space (energetically and physically) each time.
- Finish by sitting quietly for 1 minute, simply breathing.
- Honor the BIG SPIRIT that you have inside of you and vow to let Her ROAR.

FIND YOUR VOICE INTERVIEW

Take out your journal and a pen. Answer each question in a stream-of-consciousness way. Do not edit yourself. Keep your pen to paper the whole time and answer from your intuitive self. Save your answers. We will be using your responses for some upcoming leadership work.

1. What did you discover about your creative expression in this chapter?

2. What is your greatest vision for your creative expression?

3. What do you imagine are your next steps to start moving toward your greatest vision for your creative expression?

CHAPTER 9
Getting Off the Sidelines

"The world has gone too crazy. It's time for women's ways to reform."

– Jean Houston

Congratulations! You've gotten this far. You've seen how our collective history has shaped our self-image, how a male-dominated society has often squelched our ability to see ourselves as leaders, and realized that the time has come – right now – for us to step on the stage and make our voices heard.

Together we've explored your feminine creative life and seen how creative expression leads naturally to discovering your truest voice. We have met some inspiring women along the way who are using their voices for change.

This journey, I hope, has led you to a powerful revelation.

Through our work together, you've gotten a glimpse of your vision for changing the world and an opportunity to express it privately. The time has come to put all that knowledge, the inner work of self-discovery and visionary conceptualizing into action. In other words, it's time to let your inner activist meet the public.

Together in the next chapters I am going to help you create and launch a blog; I'm going to help you write a signature talk so that you can take the stage as a public speaker; and I'm going to help you put all the pieces together so you can carve out your unique pathway to trailblazing change in the 21st century.

Let's go!

CHAPTER 10
Becoming a Blogger

"I wouldn't be much of a blogger if I didn't have lots of opinions."

– Arianna Huffington

Do you have a blog? Have you thought about blogging? Are you scared to death of becoming a blogger? Since you are reading this book, I'm guessing you answered *yes* to at least one of these questions.

No matter where you fall in your responses, I'm here to tell you that becoming a blogger is one of the quickest and most accessible ways to get off the sidelines and create the change you desire to see in the world.

While male voices dominate mainstream media and key thought leader forums, blogging is a whole different story. This is where women thrive. This is where, because there is no gatekeeper, we can challenge the status quo, we can shift the conversation, and we can move the needle on most any social issue.

Take the Arab Spring, for example. Women used blogs and social media as a vital method to disseminate information and organize protests and demonstrations against the authoritarian regimes that restricted their rights in the Arab world. Since younger women were generally excluded from traditional media outlets, blogs and social media enabled them to get their message out without the filter of state-run media.

From Egypt to Saudi Arabia, from Yemen to Libya, women found their voices through blogging and social media, and used these platforms to take a stand and organize for women's rights. Now, not only are people around the world more aware of the challenges and obstacles women face in the Arab world, but the women themselves are also more aware of the rights to which they are entitled, and most importantly, are more empowered to demand these rights.

In the United States, in 2006, a handful of women came together with a desire to take on critical issues facing women, mothers and families. They wanted local, state and national leaders to understand how public policy is really affecting them and their families. They also wanted to hold corporations accountable for the fair treatment of women in the workplace. So what did they do?

They started a blog.

The group, MomsRising, went from a handful of women to now over a million members strong. Women working with the group are using the blog format to speak out about paid maternity and paternity leave, fair pay and flexible work, healthcare, affordable childcare, early childhood education, gun safety and more.

Working with their grassroots membership and state and national organizations, MomsRising has played a key role in advancing economic justice policies for women and families, including passing the Lilly Ledbetter Fair Pay Act, winning protections for pregnant workers in Maryland, winning the passage of paid family leave in Rhode Island, updating the federal nutrition standards for child care centers, and protecting key early childhood programs like Head Start.

Another group of mothers, who call themselves the MOMocrats, came together to blog about politics from a mom's perspective. Since their beginning, in 2007, the MOMocrats have pushed women's issues to the forefront of the public dialogue, connected more and more women with the political process, and their campaign, "Run, Mama Run," has been successful as publicizing and supporting the campaigns of pro-choice women candidates for elected office.

The MOMocrats are continually quoted and featured on radio, television, podcasts, and in print media, where their blogs have been syndicated by *Reuters*, *The Wall Street Journal* and *The Chicago-Sun Times*.

The blog, *Feministing*, founded by sisters Jessica and Vanessa Valenti, has given a platform to the voices of young feminists to cover a broad range of issues, including campus rape and sexual violence, street harassment, transgender rights, sexism and reproductive justice. Not only does the blog cover these issues, but it gives readers ways to take concrete actions to empower themselves and become activists. *Feministing* also provides an open-platform community where anyone – from teens to national non-profits – can make their voices heard, elevating the work of emerging feminist thinkers.

The blog has served a very important role as a gateway for young people to enter the feminist movement.

Think of Nobel Peace Prize winner and girls' global education advocate Malala Yousafzai, who started out as a blogger. At just eleven years old, Malala, from Pakistan, wrote a blog under a pseudonym, describing her life under Taliban occupation and her efforts to continue her education, despite the Taliban's ban on girls' education. Her blog was published by the BBC, and was recognized by the national and international community.

A year later, she was approached by a *New York Times* reporter about filming a documentary about her life in the

Pakistani military-occupied Swat Valley. She accepted.

Following the documentary, Malala started giving interviews to print media, on radio and on television, no longer under the pseudonym, to publicly advocate for female education. These actions led the Taliban to initiate an assassination attempt on her life. She survived, and today continues to take a stand for girls' rights to an education, and is arguably the most recognized voice and advocate for this human right.

And then of course there is Arianna Huffington, who has turned her blog, *The Huffington Post*, into the second most popular news site in the world.

When Arianna started *The Huffington Post* in 2005, she was ridiculed for creating a "silly little vanity site." While *The Huffington Post* has its share of celebrity gossip and pop triviality, it offers much more than that. It has become a place for the "voice of the people" on politics, business, social justice, women's issues, global development, environment, technology, culture, and healthy living. It has served as a platform for hundreds of women to launch their voices and opinions on social and political issues of the day onto a national and international platform. This is where I got my start.

***

There can be no doubt that blogging has changed the media world and is changing who gets to shape the conversations. If you want to become an influential leader who shapes the public dialogue, blogging is your on-ramp to achieving that.

It's important to mention that blogs take many forms, from the personal to the professional, from the purely creative to the purely informational. I am certain there is a type of blog that is just right for you.

I will work with you in this section to discover and create a blog that's right for you, where you will be able to express yourself authentically, giving voice to your message and building your visibility.

Here's a quick synopsis of the many benefits of blogging:

- Blogging gives you the power and a platform to shape the public conversation and drive national and global dialogue.

- Blogging gives you the power and a platform to bring people together and build community for a social cause or movement.

- Blogging can inform, educate, provoke, teach, inspire, challenge, promote, create and drive social and political action.

- Blogging gives you a place where you can ask people big questions, take on the complexity of issues, and empower your readers to learn from and interact with one another.

- Blogging is a critical tool for your leadership. It is a way for you to put your ideas and values into the world, and engage others in debate, conversation, and taking concrete action.

Step One: Overcoming Fear

When I started my blog, *The Goddess Diaries*, in 2008, I felt nervous about putting my voice down on paper (a.k.a. screen) for others to read. Although I had worked as a journalist 10 years earlier, I had never written in a way that was transparent about what I believed in. In other words, I had never truly expressed my own opinion.

Starting a blog felt daunting. I was concerned about exposing myself too much, and being judged for my ideas and opinions. I thought that people might think I was "too spiritual," and maybe a little bit loony tunes. I also thought that people might challenge me on my beliefs, and that felt radically scary for me.

All of those fears that I talked about in the earlier chapters showed up for me. But I started my blog anyway.

Why?

I started a blog because I felt a burning desire to make my voice heard on something that I knew was missing from the public conversation – the rise of the Divine Feminine in our cultural consciousness. I felt that if I didn't write about it, who would? I didn't think the men of media were going to cover this one.

I also felt that the human rights abuses of women and girls that I was learning about were all too quiet in mainstream media, and that I could use my voice to bring attention to these issues and drive public conversation for policy change.

While I was scared and nervous about becoming a blogger, I got myself off of the sidelines anyway. And I know you can too.

Step Two: Taking a Stand

It turns out that taking a stand for what I believed in – revealing my feminine perspective in my blog – and allowing myself to be witnessed as a writer, helped me both find and define my voice. It also created opportunity after opportunity for me to expand the reach of my voice and my influence as a feminine leader.

The first opportunity I received after starting *The Goddess Diaries* was an invitation to blog at *The Huffington Post*. This was a big deal for me, as I had only started writing my blog two months earlier. My voice had won the attention of one of the editors, and now I was being given a wider platform to expose my thinking and feminine perspective on social and political issues of the day.

With my commitment to adding a new perspective to the public conversation, I wrote weekly blogs. The frequency and consistency of my writing helped more and more people learn about me, and my blogs started to get picked up by other media platforms and publications, including Current TV, National Public Radio and *USA Today*.

I began to attend women's empowerment and leadership events, such as the California Women's Conference, the Step Up Inspiration Awards, and the United Nations Foundation Girl Up rally, reporting on the voices and good works of women and girls.

The next thing that happened is that my writing was recognized by someone at the United Nations Foundation. She recommended I apply for a press fellowship from the United Nations Foundation to report on the meetings taking place that year at United Nations General Assembly in New York City.

I was awarded this press fellowship from the United Nations Foundation, and then another one two years later.

These fellowships provided me with the opportunity to meet with world leaders, high-level officials and policy makers, global development experts, and celebrity activists to not only report on global issues affecting women and girls, but also to stir their thinking.

Now remember, this all was initiated through my decision to start *The Goddess Diaries*. It all started with a blog.

Suffice it to say that many leadership opportunities have come my way since I decided to start my blog. Most importantly, I have seen my voice make a difference.

When I started writing about these things in 2008, advancing women's leadership and addressing the human rights abuses of women and girls was not mainstream news. These things were side news. They were not considered priority importance. Over time, I have seen my voice, along with other women who have come forward to use their voice about the reality of women's lives, make a difference. We have brought these issues to the forefront so they cannot be ignored.

Every one of us who uses our voice to speak the truth of women and girls' lives and what we vision for a better future is making a difference. It won't happen without us.

Try This:
Take Your Stand

Imagine you were writing your very first blog. What would the title be?

Hint to get you started: All too often we put too much emphasis on the first blog we ever write. The trick with blogging is just to get started and not become hyper-focused on making the first blog the best thing you've ever written in your life. (My first blog was titled "How I Met My First Goddess.") If it helps, remember that each new blog you write will go on top (appear first) over older blogs. Blogging is a long-form narrative that unfolds over time. But your blogging journey will start with a single step. Take that first step now by thinking of your first blog title.

***

In my work with clients who are developing their leadership platform, blogging is a typical first step that we do together. This helps to solidify their message, activate their political voice, get them visible, and open up opportunities for them to get speaking gigs, build partnerships, and increase their influence in their area of expertise and on the issue or issues they care about most.

Take my client, Paige, for example. Paige is a New Orleans native now living in Los Angeles and a mother of three young children. Paige came to me at a time when she was struggling with finding a vision for her career and remaining on track with realistic and productive goals.

A few years prior, Paige had left her teaching job, because she didn't want to spend her children's childhood in a job that made her tired and, as she explained, was not a full expression of who she was and wanted to be in the world.

When we met, Paige was on a path to building a coaching, speaking, writing and teaching career. The problem was, she had so many ideas swirling around in her mind, that without a guide, she felt alone with them, unable to see how they connected, and unable to organize them in a way that gave voice to her message. She said she spent time "thinking" so much about her ultimate vision and business that it felt like she was "doing" a lot, but she wasn't actually getting a lot done. Paige was full of hesitation and self-doubt.

In order to help Paige organize her thoughts, get clear on her vision, overcome her self-doubt, give voice to her message, and start building her business, I suggested Paige start by writing a blog.

Paige courageously jumped in. As she wrote, she dug into her message, and discovered the political and change-agent perspective she naturally has, but wasn't owning before. As she wrote, she became infused with courage, was making faster decisions, and was owning her message about honoring the truth of women's lives.

After writing her first few blogs, Paige started creating her course offerings, workshops and coaching programs. Her vision for her business became clear.

Blogging not only became a platform for Paige to share her expertise and unique perspective she has on women's lives, it also became an incredible way for Paige to offer healing and courage to the women she serves.

She began to grow a mailing list, was contacted by other blogs, such as *The Huffington Post*, to write for them, and now has women coming to her classes and signing up for her workshops because they found her through her blog.

Paige told me that she always considered herself a writer, privately, but that blogging has been her way to claim her creativity and step into the world as an artist. As Paige's business grows and expands, she is now receiving speaking opportunities.

Try this:

How Often Should You Write?

Blogging every single day is a challenge. But you can set yourself a schedule of blogging once a week. What would that look like for you?

Consider your time, and when you would blog. Copy down the lists below and circle the options that make the most sense for you.

I would blog:

- every day
- once a week
- every two weeks
- once a month

My best time for writing is:

- first thing in the morning
- on my lunch hour
- late at night
- I don't have a good time for writing (more about that problem later)

As a woman, when you get out there with a blog, you get to take a stand for what you believe in. There is no one editing you. No one restricting you. No one inhibiting you. In short, there is no gatekeeper. You are free to use your voice as you wish. This is revolutionary.

Let's start your revolution.

***

Step Three: Your Blogging Action Plan

We are now going to put all of the work you did in the Find Your Voice Interviews into action. Remember when I told you to save your responses in your journal because we were going to use them for some upcoming leadership work? Well, here we are. You've arrived.

Here are the steps I recommend to streamline your process of starting a blog.

Choose Your First Blog Post Topic. I've already had you thinking about this. Now let's build it out a little. Go back to your Find Your Voice Interview responses from Chapter 5 (Using Your Voice for Social Justice), and brainstorm five blog post titles that address the social injustice you feel most emotionally charged by. Then circle one title that feels most on target with where your voice and energy are right now.

Get Clear on Your Audience. It is important to know who you are writing your blog for because otherwise, why write it? The best way to reach your audience is to be clear about who you are writing for. That way your voice will come through most naturally, and your argument will be easier to make. Are you writing for the people you want to help (see Chapter 1's Find Your Voice Interview responses)? Are you writing for people who you want to join a movement? Are you writing for the policymakers who you want to take action to implement your political vision (see Chapter 4's Find Your Voice Interview responses)? If you're having trouble thinking of your audience, write out a few profiles as though you were compiling a dossier on each person. Even if made up (fictional), these will help you visualize your audience. You can also base them on real people.

Decide What You Want Your Audience to Do. This will make your blog writing and your life that much easier. What do you want your readers to do after they finish reading your blog? Write their legislators? Join a movement? Take a self-care or personal development action? When you know what you want your audience to do at the end of your blog, your blog will be that much stronger.

Write a First Draft. Now it's time to get out your pen (or computer) and write a first draft. Choose whichever modality invites your most authentic voice. Just like you did in the Find Your Voice Interviews, let this first draft be a stream-of-consciousness writing. Get all of your thoughts and feelings down in this first draft. Give yourself permission to be as messy as you need to be. Just get things down.

The Second Draft. Give yourself some time and space between your first draft and second draft, even if it's just an hour. As a start to your second draft, re-read your first draft and pay special attention to the "energized themes." Map out a strategy to present your thoughts, feelings and storytelling to take readers to the end point (action step) that you want them to get to.

Tip: You don't have to adhere to a rigid structure in your blog writing, but know that your reader will be looking for some kind of structure to help carry them through your writing. Your blog may shape itself into one of these kinds of structure:

- a personal story
- a journalistic narrative
- an interview[2]
- a tips or tools list

All of these are valid structures for a blog. Sometimes, you can even combine different kinds. (I often combine a personal story with a journalistic narrative.) Be aware of structure as you write, because you know that your reader will.

---

[2] If you are less of a writer, but more of a talker, try doing an interview format. Interview a mentor, someone who inspires you, or a colleague who is doing good work. Have it transcribed inexpensively by a service like speechpad.com and post it to your blog.

Once you have written your second draft, read through it and 1) be sure it stays on topic; 2) check if it sticks to the structure you set out, or if you need to change the structure; and 3) make any copy edits that are needed.

Give Your Draft to a Reader. Once you've gotten your blog in good shape, have a friend, family member, coach or colleague whose writing skills and opinion you trust review your blog. Ask them to give you feedback to encourage you, as well as help you strengthen the blog. (Tip: Your blog does not have to be "perfect" before handing it on to your reader. Do the best you can, and then move it on for feedback.)

Not everyone has the luxury of having a trusted reader on hand, but if you do, I highly recommend it. If you can't get anybody to read your work, or you don't want them to, try reading your blog out loud to yourself, or try a text-to-speech application (Mac computers come with this app built in) so that you can hear your blog being read to you. At the very least, it will help you catch typos.

Finalize Your Blog. Finalize your blog post, incorporating the feedback you received, only making the changes that you feel strengthen the blog. Comments and feedback are great, but you have to be true to yourself. You have to recognize constructive criticism and discard negative criticism. This is a skill that develops over time as you develop your writing voice.

Post Your Blog. If you have not already, go to Wordpress.com[3] and register your blog. This is where you will make all of your blog posts. Come up with a name for your overall blog that represents your political vision (see Chapter 4's Find Your Voice Interview responses). An alternative is to come up with a title that represents what you stand for and inspires you to write on a frequent basis.

Additional notes on names: A unique name is important because the name of your blog is the primary way people will find it when they search in Google, Bing or Yahoo. But don't stress if you can't get the name you want. (It might be already taken.) Aside from the name, you'll have another opportunity to make your blog stand out in search results – with your description. This is a block of text that appears just below the name of the blog that gives your readers a preview of what it's about.

Once you've got your blog registered, make your first post.

Share with the Public. Send out an email to your friends, family and colleagues to let them know about your newly launched blog, and invite them to read it, comment on it, and share it with their networks. Or send out an email to your newsletter list, if you have one. Strategize on how you will use social media to reach the audience you want to reach. (See below for guidance on how to do this.) There is a whole science built around growing your readership. What I'm providing here is just the basics to get you started.

---

[3] I prefer Wordpress, but you could also try Blogger, the original blogging platform, or Tumblr.

The WordPress Community

If you have put your blog on WordPress, there is a built-in community waiting to discover you there. They will find you by the title of your blog, and your description. They will also find you by the tags you attach to your blog. Tags are short descriptive phrases or single words that you can associate with your blog to help readers who are interested in your topic to discover you faster.

Depending on what you are writing about, you will want to tag your blog with words like: women, feminist, political, creative, family, activist, or whatever phrase or word you think fits.

You can get a taste of how this works by checking out this link: http://wordpress.com/tags/

Social Media

You probably have a social media platform that you enjoy using the most. It might be Facebook, Twitter, Instagram or Pinterest. Since you like using it, you have discovered friends there. That platform is the one you should get started on with posting links to your blog. Whenever you write a blog, post a link to it on your favorite platform, along with a short introduction. If you're using Facebook, for example, you might provide some context about why you wrote it, what it was like to write, or ask for feedback about it.

Get Some Air. Go for a walk and give yourself some breathing space. Believe it or not, this is helpful for the dissemination of your blog.

Frequently Asked Blogging Questions

Q: How long should my blog be?

A: Somewhere around 500 words is a good length. Readers can typically pay attention for this length of text.

Q: *Do I need to post a picture with my blog?*

A: Pictures help readers get started reading, particularly if you are posting a link to your blog on Facebook, which is a visual medium. But don't let the lack of a picture hold you back. Many successful blogs do well without any images at all.

Q: *Where can I find free images and graphics for my blog?*

A: http://search.creativecommons.org is a good source. You can also use Google's advanced image search to find images that are free to use:
http://www.google.com/advanced_image_search

Q: *How far in advance should I write my blog? Should I try to write every day?*

A: This is a personal choice. If you are inspired to write something every day, go for it. My suggestion is to start with writing a blog a week at first. By all means, start a list of topics you'd like to cover, and start writing each one when it moves you. If you get stuck on one topic and can't go on with it, come back to it later and try another on your list.

Alternative Forms of Blogging

If writing isn't your thing, but you want to have a foundation for your larger platform, do not despair. There are other forms of blogging that you can explore.

Vlogging

A vlog (video blog or video log) is a form of a blog for which the medium is video. The people who make these are typically known as vloggers. This has become an incredibly popular form of communication with people creating their own YouTube channels.

Vlogging, like blogging, is an extremely powerful social change tool because in order to make and publish your own videos, you don't need permission from any male-dominated media conglomerate, corporation, government, or religion. Your feminine values and creativity are at the center here. You have complete creative control. This is *huge*.

Photo Blogging

Are images moving to you? Post a stream of photographs that represents what you stand for on Flickr, Tumblr, Instagram or WordPress.

Music Blogging

If music is your medium of expression, post your latest creations to soundcloud.com. There is a vibrant community of musicians there, and spoken word pieces also.

Try this:

FEMININE LEADERSHIP PRACTICE

Step into your sacred space and set your timer for 2 minutes.

Liberating Your Voice. As someone new to blogging, you may be experiencing some panic right about now. Can I really write about what's tugging at my soul? Can I really be outspoken about all these things I care about deeply? Am I ready to do this?

Physically, you may even be feeling some constriction around your throat. If you are not experiencing any of this, then more power to you. Keep going. If you are, however, please know that you are not alone. All of this is quite common for women who are blazing a new path. Today's leadership practice is designed to help you move beyond any physical and emotional restrictions you might feel around your throat and put you on a path to liberating your voice.

- Sit comfortably in your sacred space in your meditation position.
- Soften your eyes.
- Inhale and exhale through your nose a few times.
- On your next breath, let out a lion's roar, sticking your tongue out really far. (You did this practice back in Chapter 8.) Repeat the lion's roar three times.
- Next, start to make as many funny faces as you can with your mouth. Open your mouth as wide as you can vertically, then horizontally. Scrunch up your mouth. Pucker your lips. Do some kisses. Just keep moving your mouth in as many shapes as you can.
- Start to transition your mouth shapes into a yawn. Open your mouth wide and let out some yawning sounds. Let the yawns come. Allow whatever sound that wants to release with the yawn, to release.
- From here, start to transition your yawn sounds to sighs. Invite your body to move as it wishes as you let out some sighs. Try not to judge the sounds coming out of you. Just give them some breathing room to release.
- Now, transition your sighs into groans. Here is where I want you to really go for it. Groaning, like growling, is a primal sound. It connects you to your natural power. Allow your body to move as it wishes as you groan. Groan. Groan. And groan some more. Let it out. Try not to judge the sounds coming out of you. Be curious about them, and notice how your body is activated as you groan.

Next, transition your groans into laughter. Ha, ha,

ha, ha, ha, ha. Even if you have to fabricate a laugh, start that way. Allow yourself to smile as you laugh. Allow your body open up as you laugh. Even if you feel a little kooky (you probably will), keep laughing. Give yourself permission to feel laughter in your heart and throughout your body. Move as your body wishes. Let the laughter come.

- Notice what the laughter has to teach you. What is happening at your throat? Is there joy? Is there sadness? Is there something that wants to be said? Be with what is there. Give yourself space to liberate what is getting activated in your throat chakra. (A chakra is an energy center in your body.)

- Breathe.

- Take a few deep breaths and slowly allow your mind and body to settle. Drop your energy and attention down to your hips and feel into where you are sitting. Get grounded. Breathe.

- Slowly draw your hands up toward your neck, and place your hands lovingly around your neck. Send some love to your throat chakra. (Your throat chakra is the energy center that is related to your ability to communicate and create.)

- Move your hands toward the back of your neck, then to the sides of your neck, and then return to the front, breathing deeply as you go and nourishing this area that is in direct relationship with your voice and self-expression.

- Vow to listen to your voice and continually nourish Her with practices like the one you did today.

- Finish by sounding one OM.

FIND YOUR VOICE INTERVIEW

Take out your journal and a pen. Set a timer for 1 minute for each question. Answer each question in a stream-of-consciousness way. Do not edit yourself. Keep your pen to paper the whole time. Give yourself permission to truly express yourself.

1. What do you feel scared to talk about on a public platform?

2. In your heart of hearts, what do you want to blog about?

3. What, if anything, do you feel would stop you from using your voice for what you believe in?

CHAPTER 11
Becoming a Public Speaker

"It took me quite a long time to develop a voice, and now that I have it, I am not going to be silent."

– Madeleine Albright

The imposter syndrome. You know that feeling, right? *I'm here. But I don't really belong here. Someone else is clearly more qualified than me.* I have had so many clients run into this along their path to becoming a public speaker, and I have certainly experienced this too.

I want to share with you that it took me a long time to get the courage to go out and be a public speaker. One factor was the imposter syndrome, and another was the fact that I was spinning around the question of what I *specifically* wanted to share with women. Sound familiar?

While it was clear to me that my work – my calling – was to empower the voices of women and girls, I felt confused about the best way to do that. Should I do it through a talk about divine assignments? Should I do it through a talk about helping women find their political voice? Should I do it through a talk about feminine spirituality being the missing link to women's leadership?

How could I go out there and be a public speaker if I didn't know what I wanted to say?

I struggled and struggled. For a long time, I felt on the verge of being ready to give a signature talk – a talk that represented my core message, that would help me advance the status of what I stand for, and also establish me as a leading expert in my field. But I wondered if I had the credibility to be out there giving those talks, and if I had the courage to stand in the spotlight.

Over time, this changed for me, and I got out there with my first signature talk, *How to Find Your Political Voice*, to an auditorium full of professional women seeking greater leadership and influence in their careers and their community. I had a blast. I also discovered that the anticipation of giving a talk is a lot more anxiety producing than actually giving the talk.

After I spoke, a young woman came right up to me to thank me for inspiring her and told me about her dream to work with the United Nations. I was excited to hear more and engaged with her in conversation for a couple of minutes. Before I knew it, I was tapped on the shoulder by the public relations manager of the organization that had hired me to speak. She pointed her finger to the line of women that had formed behind me. Apparently, they were all waiting to talk with me.

This was a huge paradigm shift that took me a moment to absorb. I was usually the one waiting in line.

Not only was giving this talk a ton of fun, it was also great income. When the organization invited me to speak, I set a strong speaking fee, including travel and expenses. I knew that what I had to offer was valuable and so was my time. While the organization didn't have a large budget up front, they were able to honor my speaking fee by seeking sponsorship for the event. It was a win-win-win for everyone.

Thank goodness I took my first step into public speaking with a signature talk because public speaking has brought me a much bigger platform for my ideas and continues to open up opportunities for me to reach more and more women and girls.

In this chapter, we're going to work together to bring you the clarity and courage you need to create *your signature talk*.

***

If you are already out there as a public speaker, I'm delighted to hear this. Keep going.

I'm guessing, however, that there are others of you that have public speaking aspirations, but self-doubt, procrastination and self-sabotage keep getting in the way. I've seen this many times over with my clients, and as you just heard, this was also my story.

If you happen to be one of the few who think that public speaking is not important and don't see the need for it on your leadership path, I want to challenge you on that. Please keep reading.

***

Let's first dive into why having a signature talk is important.

5 Great Things That Will Happen When You Have a Signature Talk

Once you have activated your political voice and have built self-confidence through blog writing, then it's time to start to transmit your message through the spoken word. This is the next step to amplify your influence on the social and political issues that you care about most. In short: it's the next step to owning your power.

Here are five great things that will happen when you have your signature talk:

1. **You will empower other women and girls.** When you step on stage as a leader speaking about the change you are here to create in the world, you not only empower yourself, you empower all women and girls around the world. You become a role model, and girls everywhere can begin to see themselves on stage as leaders, confidently speaking and delivering an important message to improve the well-being of our world.

2. **You will shift the balance of power.** As we've talked about so much in this book, women's voices are all too absent in leadership positions and in all the places that have influence on our laws and public policies. When you use your voice to speak about the change you are here to create in the world, you step into leadership and help shift the balance of power to move us in the direction of partnership with men and the masculine.

3. **You will improve the human rights of women and girls.** As you help shift the balance of power toward a partnership between the feminine and the masculine, the atrocities that women and girls are currently experiencing every day around the world, including rape, sexual slavery, domestic abuse, forced child marriage, genital mutilation, infanticide and outright murder, will start to dissipate.

Shining your light on these topics will make them more difficult to sustain. By stepping on stage as a public speaker and embodying feminine leadership, you contribute to moving us out of a misogynistic system.

4. **You will speed up the rate of social and political change**. When you stand on stage and give your signature talk – whether it's a national or international event with 3,000 people, or a local event with 10 people – you are mobilizing others to get on board with creating the change that you envision for the world. The people who come to hear you talk – whether they are women or men – will be drawn to you because you are putting a stake in the ground and coming full out with YOUR TRUTH. Your truth is the cause you were born for. When you speak openly and honestly about this, the people who need to find you *will* find you. They may become your clients, your business partners, or fellow activists or advocates. By putting your stake in the ground with your signature talk, you will quickly be growing and speeding up the rate by which you want to create change.

5. **You will increase your influence and enjoy more income.** This last thing is a very practical one. Once you have your signature talk ready to go and you are out there giving it, you will be recognized as a leading expert in your field, increase your influence and enjoy more income. Some of the benefits in this regard include: receiving invitations to speak and participate at influential conferences, to the media, and at prominent events; reaching tens of thousands of people with your message; enjoying a steady stream of clients; enjoying more income; and ultimately making the big impact in the world you know you were born for. How can you turn all of that down?

Now that you have five outstanding reasons to create a signature talk, let's dive into how you are going to do this.

Different Approaches to Writing a Signature Talk

Sometimes it is helpful to know exactly where you want to give your talk before you even start to put anything down on paper. That way you know the expectations, the length of the talk, and the protocol. This, however, is not the method for everyone. Some of you may need to start writing before you identify the specifics of where you want to give your talk.

The steps in the following exercise will help you establish the foundation of your signature talk, and will give you the flexibility to lengthen or shorten your talk, according to the time frame of your venue, and modify your talk as needed to match your exact audience.

Ready to get your signature talk down on paper?

10 STEPS TO WRITE YOUR SIGNATURE TALK

I suggest doing these steps over a two-day period. On day one, do steps 1 – 6. On day two, do steps 7 – 10.

DAY ONE:

STEP 1: Have Some Compassion for Yourself. Acknowledge the collective consciousness and unconsciousness around women stepping forward as speakers and messengers of their Truth. (Remember Chapter 7 – Breaking Through Visibility Fears?) When it comes to being a public speaker, give yourself permission to release any shame around "Not having done it yet."

STEP 2: Identify Your Audience. Remember all the exercises you did earlier in the book to get clear on the change you want to create and the people you want to help? Refer back to those and identify who you want to speak to, in order to be the most effective in creating the change you are here to make. Do you want to speak to lawmakers, media-makers, mothers, corporate women, at-risk youth, domestic abuse survivors, entrepreneurs, teachers, artists, religious leaders, . . . you get the point. Identify your audience and write this down.

STEP 3: Activate Your Empathy. Pretend you're about to give your talk. Take 30 seconds to write down how your audience might be feeling just before you are about to speak. What questions can you ask them to let them know you "see them" and understand how they feel? Now, take another 30 seconds to write down how you imagine they *want* to feel. What questions can you ask them to let them know that you understand their dreams and desires? This information will help you tremendously as you move forward with creating your talk.

STEP 4: Choose Your Topic. Remember the list of blog topics that you brainstormed in the previous chapter? Do any of those titles strike you as a title for a signature talk? (FYI: you can have more than one signature talk, but we will focus on just one in this chapter.) Choose a title and topic that you have the most energy around right now that would be a terrific vehicle for you to deliver your message to your audience, inspire them and move them into action.

STEP 5: Set the Intention of Your Signature Talk. Remember back in Chapter 4 when you activated your political voice? Check back in with your responses to the Find Your Voice Interview in that chapter and spend a few minutes breathing into and connecting with your bigger mission. (Connecting to that bigger mission can help you move through some visibility issues that may be showing up right about now.) Again, visualize yourself on stage, this time at the beginning of your talk. Then with your pen and paper do a stream-of-consciousness writing (30 seconds), filling in this sentence: *My intention here today is to . . .*

STEP 6: Write the Closing of Your Signature Talk

I'm putting this step here so that you can create the container for your talk. Doing this step early on will help make the process of writing the body of your signature talk *much easier*. So now, visualize yourself on stage in front of your audience at the *end* of your talk. Remember how they felt in the beginning of your talk and how you identified they wanted to feel by the end of your talk. Then with your pen and paper, do a stream-of-consciousness writing (30 seconds), filling in this sentence: *I hope you will walk away from today with . . .*

Now take a breath and break for today.

DAY TWO:

STEP 7: Identify the Transformation. First, identify the problem you are addressing with your talk. Second, identify the solution you are offering. Then, in a stream-of-consciousness writing (2 minutes), tell your audience how your signature talk topic relates to them and how your talk can help them. You may want to include some details about how they may be feeling before your talk, and how they will feel afterwards. You've already done some of this work in the earlier steps.

STEP 8: Establish Your Teaching Points. Brainstorm five teaching points that you'd like to offer your audience in relation to your signature talk topic. Once you have these, narrow the teaching points down to three. Once you have your three teaching points established, do a stream-of-consciousness writing for each teaching point (2 minutes each), including the "juice" of what you want them to learn and how they can apply this to their lives and empower themselves to solve the problem your talk is addressing.

STEP 9: Include Stories for Your Teaching Points. Stories reach people's hearts and minds and help build community. According to current research, stories stimulate and engage your listeners, helping the speaker connect with the audience and making it much more likely that the audience will agree with your point of view. Come up with a story for two of your teaching points.

STEP 10: Own Your Story and Expertise. Do a stream-of-consciousness writing (2 minutes) about how you relate to your audience. What have you felt that they are probably feeling? What experiences have you had that may be similar to their experiences? Do you have a "mess to success story" or "story of transformation" related to your signature talk topic? What is your personal connection to this topic? How do you relate to your audience? Once you've done this, then make a list of your credentials that establish your credibility on this topic. Include both personal and professional. You aren't necessarily going to include this list in your talk, but it's good for you to have the experience of writing this down in one spot so you can synthesize it as a way to more deeply own your expertise.

Surprise! There's one more step (very important) …

STEP 11: Move Your Audience into Action. What do you want your audience to do at the end of your talk? Brainstorm three action steps. Sit with these a moment. Then choose one action step that feels the most doable and accessible for your audience, so that they will actually take action. Your focus will help them focus. You could say something like, "If you do one thing after this talk today, . . ." Conclude with what you hope they learned/got from the talk, and if they want to go further, how you can support them.

Hooray! You've created the foundation for your signature talk. Congratulations. This is big work.

Now what?

***

It's time to organize your talk.

If you did the previous exercise, you have all of the parts of your talk written out and available to you. Now it's time to put them together into a talk that will educate, engage, inspire and move your audience into action to help them achieve their (and your) dreams.

But how do you decide the flow?

The first thing to consider here is that the most inspiring speakers tend to be the ones who are open, authentic and, at times, vulnerable. This gives you credibility, and a soul connection with the audience.

Secondly, humor is always a good thing to call on during your talk. While your topic might be serious, it's a good idea to have some moments where you lighten up and not take yourself, or your topic, so seriously. Research shows that humor lowers defenses, making your audience more receptive to your message. It also makes you seem more likeable, and people are more willing to support the ideas of someone they like. Tip: You don't necessarily need to tell a joke to get a laugh.

So let's look at a format for you to follow to help you lay out your signature talk. It may not be the final structure you will use for your talk, as I talk about later, but it will provide you with a firm foundation to work from.

Organizing Your Signature Talk

I have provided a template below for you to work from. This is where you can plug in all of the work you did from the "10 Steps" exercise. There will be some additional steps to take, as you'll see below, but for the most part, you've done all of the work already. Have fun!

TITLE
subtitle

You may start with a certain title, but change it later after you've laid out your talk. Sometimes there's more clarity after working through the different sections of the talk. For now, brainstorm three subtitles that tell people what they will get from your talk so that they'll want to get their ticket for entry.

SECTION 1: Establish a relationship with your audience. Show them you "get" them. Here are some ways to do this. You can choose one, two, or all three:

- **Ask questions to get them grounded into why they are there**. For example: How many of you have ever . . .? How many of you have longed to . . .? How many of you . . .? Ask two or three questions that apply to your audience. By the end of the questions you want everyone in your audience to have raised their hand.

- **Share some statistics about your topic to awaken your audience to the urgency of your message.** For example: Did you know that an estimated _____ women in the U.S. suffer from . . .?

- **Make a universal statement that they can connect with to let them know you are speaking to them. Get them to do some critical thinking.** (i.e., Is that true?) For example: It doesn't have to be so hard to live your professional purpose and make your greatest contributions while still putting your kids first. . . .

Remember that humor can break the ice and help your audience connect with you, getting them ready to listen to what you have to say. As I mentioned earlier, this doesn't necessarily mean telling a joke, but sharing something that gets them to laugh or smile, even if your topic is a serious one.

SECTION 2: In no more than three sentences, tell your audience what you are going to talk to them about and what your intention is for the talk.

SECTION 3: Share your story. Look at the major elements of your life that made you want to give this talk to your audience. What happened in your life that inspires you to give this talk? What was the tipping point that made you say: *I have to do this.* Write out your story in broad strokes. Tip: Don't go into too much detail, just get the arc of the story so we understand your path and why you are the one talking to us about this topic.

SECTION 4: Affirm for the audience that they are in the right place listening to your talk. For example, you are in the right place if you . . .

- Are experiencing . . .
- Don't want to settle for . . .
- Desire to . . .

Take some time to get into your audience's shoes. Come up with five statements to affirm for them that they are in the right place listening to your talk. You won't necessarily use all five of these, but they will be helpful for you to have in your back pocket.

SECTION 5: Educate your audience about your topic. What is it? Why is it important? What is the problem? What is your solution? Are there any jaw-dropping facts or anecdotes that your audience should know about it?

SECTION 6: Give your audience three tools to help them become empowered around this topic and to become part of the solution. This is where I suggest sharing an anecdote or two to help the audience have an intimate connection with one or two of the tools. They will remember these better. Note: These don't have to be called "tools." Some other words you might consider are *lessons learned, practices, action steps,* and so forth. Use what feels right for you and your topic.

SECTION 7: Make a Call to Action. What do you want your audience to do?

SECTION 8: Conclude with what you hope they learned, what they will walk away with, and what your deepest wish is for them as they move forward.

END

After you plug in all of your material into this template, read it from beginning to end. As you do this, feel into whether any section wants to be moved to another spot. Find your flow. Trust your intuition and inner authority. This is your signature talk. *Remember to circle back to your title and subtitle and see if any changes need to be made.

***

I want to take a moment to point out here that while many women get started blogging before writing a signature talk, sometimes the sequence goes the other way.

Take my client Rachel, for instance. Rachel is from North Carolina, has a marketing and communications background, and is a wife and mom to two girls.

She came to me while she was working at a corporate job, and told me she was feeling burnt out and out of place in that setting. She told me she saw a need for more feminine leadership and feminine values in the business world, and in leadership positions in general worldwide. She wanted to do something about this.

The problem was that Rachel had been struggling for awhile because her vision was so grand for what was possible, that she wasn't sure where to begin.

In order to find her voice on this topic and develop her language around the issue, as well as to build her confidence to take on this leadership, we started Rachel on writing a signature talk.

This made sense for Rachel because she saw herself speaking at corporations and at large conference venues.

Within five weeks of working together, Rachel had completed writing her signature talk, "Why There Aren't More Women in Leadership and How We Can Change This." She also had a game plan for securing speaking engagements, had an ally in Washington, D.C. help her get connected with a number of groups to expand her social footprint, and developed a relationship with two groups internationally who expressed interest in collaborating on a project to increase the prominence of women leaders.

Rachel also created an outline for her first book, on feminine leadership.

With all these elements, Rachel had the blueprint for her new business, the New Vision Project, an organization dedicated to increasing the prominence of women leaders around the globe. She launched her business five months later, along with her website and blog. Rachel's first guest blog post was featured on the home page of ModernMom.com.

For Rachel, writing a signature talk was the foundation she needed to launch her bigger leadership platform. Her blog came later. *The sequence might go that way for you, too.*

How Long Should My Signature Talk Be?

I get this question a lot from my clients. The answer is: it depends on where you give your talk. Every venue has a different requirement or request for the length of your talk.

TED Talks, for example, should be no longer than 18 minutes. TED curator Chris Anderson has been quoted saying 18 minutes is "long enough to be serious and short enough to hold people's attention."

Social Good Summit (in New York City) talks typically are 12 – 15 minutes. South by Southwest Festival talks range from 15 minutes to one hour, depending on the session category. I had a client speak at the Women in Cable Television Leadership Conference, and they asked her to prepare a talk that was just 10 minutes.

Speaking at a university, however, is typically a longer talk. For instance, when I spoke at Boise State University, they asked me to speak for one hour. I was the plenary speaker. I had a client speak at New York University, and she spoke for 45 minutes. Another client spoke at a psychology conference at a university in the mid-west and she was asked to speak for 30 minutes.

My suggestion is to write out a first draft of your talk that times out to be about 20 minutes. From there, you can adjust it to be shorter or longer, as needed. Just be aware that researchers have discovered that "cognitive backlog" (too much information) prevents the successful transmission of ideas. That argues for talks that are shorter rather than longer, talks with stories that listeners can connect with, rather than a cascade of facts, and a personal approach that lets your audience connect with you as an individual.

So, during your 20 minutes on stage, make sure you:

- Connect intimately and authentically with your audience
- Emotionally engage them
- Tell a few stories
- Teach them a few things
- Move them into action

You can do this!

To Practice or Not to Practice?

I recommend practicing your talk *a lot*. Don't just read it through one or two times and try to hop on stage. This will be crazy making. Practicing your talk over and over will help you to internalize your content so that when you are up on stage, you can deliver the presentation as comfortably as having a conversation with a close friend.

Here are some tips for practicing:

- Practice your talk on your own at the start. Get comfortable with the flow. Get the language into your body and start to find an ease with articulating the words you have written.

- Record yourself giving your talk either through your iPhone, your computer, or a video camera. This will help you get used to "being seen" giving your talk, as well as provide you with audio and visual data to help you improve upon the delivery of your talk.

- Give your talk to a friend, spouse, mentor or colleague. Ask them for constructive feedback. How did they feel at the beginning of the talk? How did they feel at the end of the talk? Was there any part of the talk that didn't make sense to them? Did they want clarity in any particular areas? What moved them? Do they feel motivated to take action?

To Memorize or Not to Memorize?

Many clients ask whether they should memorize their talk or whether it's okay for them to use notes or notecards. My opinion on this is that it depends on who you are and how you will feel standing on stage without any notes. Do think you might freeze up and forget your speech entirely as you step on stage? Do you feel you might lose your way without the notes? If so, then I think notes are a good idea. You may end up never using them, or only referring to them a couple of times during your talk. If they give you the confidence to get out there, then I say bring them.

Nonetheless, I do think you should memorize your talk. If you follow the practice tips in the previous section, then you will be well on your way to memorizing your talk.

The reason I suggest this is because memorizing your talk will allow you to be in the moment and more spontaneous when up on stage. You will be able to connect with your audience at a deeper level when you know you've done your practice and embodied your talk. You will be able to better respond to the people who are right there in front of you on that given day. This matters. This is how your audience will begin to know, like and trust you.

When you are present, you can "see" them and, when they feel seen, they will listen to you.

Developing Your Stage Presence

Stage presence matters. It can mean the difference between people listening to you, trusting what you have to say, and getting on board with what you are proposing or advocating, *and* people not listening to you, not finding you credible, and wishing they were somewhere else during those 20 minutes.

Something that comes up for women time and time again is the question: "What should I do with my body when I'm on stage?" It's a good question and one that has a simple answer, but is not always easy to achieve: be relaxed and move how you naturally want to move.

Since so many of us have been socialized to not take up too much space, when we get up on stage, we tend to literally not take up much space. This is a real killer for your talk.

When you step on stage as a speaker, the audience is looking to you as an authority. They want you to take up space, be a leader and guide them to a new insight, discovery or action plan. If you shrink in the spotlight, you deflate their hope and inspiration, and also your credibility.

So, my recommendation to my clients (and I do this myself) is to practice your talk with exaggerated physical movements. Think: overstated hand movements and gestures, frequent smiling, and moving around the stage in a grand way to own the space.

While this may feel silly and disingenuous at the time, it's really a great practice to help you get over physical inhibitions and help you own the space. You'll notice in this practice that your voice will become more powerful too. While you won't necessarily give your talk with the exaggerated gestures, by the time you get on stage you'll know what it feels like to truly own the space, and you'll be more likely to show up physically, mentally and emotionally at ease.

What about supporting materials, like Keynotes or PowerPoints?

Clients often ask if I recommend using these, and if so, how should they do them? My feeling is that for a lot of talks they are not necessary. If they don't serve a greater purpose to your talk, then skip it. In some cases, however, a PowerPoint or Keynote is the way to go. Some audiences need visuals.

While a lot of people think of PowerPoints as bullet points, they don't have to be that — and in fact, I recommend you stay away from bullet points. What I do recommend is communicating with your audience by putting up slides of images that evoke what you're talking about. This can be a very effective way to emotionally engage your audience, and give them a powerful, memorable experience.

Now that you've got a draft of your signature talk, and you've been practicing it relentlessly, it's time to get cracking and start giving your talk.

Here are some easy steps to follow to book yourself some speaking engagements:

- Make a list of places where you want to give your talk. (Refer back to the target audience you identified in "10 Steps to Create Your Signature Talk.") Where are those people? What conferences do they attend? What groups or organizations do they belong to? What events do they participate in? In short, where do they gather?

- Make a list that includes at least five venues. (When you are first getting going, a venue could be something as small as a boutique gallery, book store or hair salon where you can gather a small crowd one evening.)

- From your list, circle the places where you already have personal connections.

- Send an email to those personal connections to let them know that you are now giving your signature talk and that you'd like to speak with them about the possibility of presenting to their audience.

- Research the other organizations, groups and conferences where you'd like to speak. (I have included a comprehensive list of my favorite women's conferences later in this chapter.) If you want to go beyond that list, Google "women's conferences call for speakers 2015" (or whatever year you are looking for) to bring up a list of the most current calls for speakers, or check out the TEDx conferences coming up in your area. Also, check LinkedIn groups for women's groups and speakers groups. They will give you leads.

- Find out who to contact at each one to have a conversation about presenting your talk to their audience. Tip: Many women's conferences have a "How to Apply to Be a Speaker" button on their website. You can fill out the application, send it in, and, if you have any personal connections at those conferences, make sure to reach out to them and ask them to put in a good word for you. (Remember to use LinkedIn or any other professional groups to which you may belong to help you with this.)

Creating a Speaker Page

When you apply to be a speaker at a conference, pitch your signature talk to a prospective venue, or reach out to your personal and professional connections to let them know you are looking for support to book some speaking gigs, you're going to need to have somewhere to send them so they can learn about you as a public speaker. Ideally, this will be a speaker page on your website. If you don't have a website at the moment, don't worry. I have an alternative option for you coming up.

For those of you with a website, your speaker page should include:

- A downloadable headshot. Be sure to include one that you would want others to use in publicizing your talk. If you have a high-quality one of you speaking somewhere, even better. That helps your page visitors envision you on their stage. If not, no worries. Just include one that helps visitors "get to know" you.

- A short paragraph describing you, your mission, and your work. Include here a few credentials that show you as an expert on the topic(s) you speak about.

- Testimonials that brag about you and/or shine a spotlight on how you have touched people's lives. If you have testimonials about you as a presenter or speaker, those are the best to use. If you don't have any of those yet because you are a first-time speaker, no worries. Use whatever exemplifies the potency of how you have affected people's lives (clients, colleagues, students).

- A list of other places where you have previously spoken. If you don't have anything to include here yet, just skip this for now. You'll build this as you go.

- A video showing you speaking. This is extremely helpful for anyone who is considering booking you for their audience. If you are just getting started as a speaker, you most likely don't have this. An alternative would be to make a short video (2 minutes) on your iPhone or video camera, talking on your topic and sharing your passion for it. Please make sure that the lighting and sound are high-quality in this video. Otherwise, it's best to keep off the video for now.

If you don't have a website yet, you can make a speaker page another way, and it's free. A really quick way to do this is through a service called about.me. You can send people to this page, which will describe your topics and abilities, as you are getting a more formal speaker page setup.

Women's Conferences in the United States

The women's conference industry is growing, and, according to labor statistics, is expected to balloon over the next five years. There are conferences for entrepreneurs, corporate women, moms, philanthropists, activists, bloggers, spiritual seekers, foodies, women in tech, environmentalists, innovators, teen girls, abuse survivors, and more.

As Jessica Bennett reported in the *New York Times* earlier this year, there are conferences out of which movements have grown, such as Sheryl Sandberg's "Lean In," which began as a talk at TEDWomen. There are also those that aim to create movements, such as Politico's Women Rule conference. Their tagline is, "Innovating a Movement."

These conferences serve as gathering spots for women to discuss the issues of the day, discuss what is important to them and be taken seriously. "It's part of every social justice movement," said Gloria Steinem in an interview, last year, at the Makers Conference in Southern California.

When women come together at these conferences working toward a common cause, that's when change gets put into motion. Wouldn't it be great to be an active change agent in this way?

***

Here are some of the most largely attended conferences where you may want to set your sights on speaking in the future. I have listed them in chronological order. Please note, however, that the dates are subject to change from year to year.

The MAKERS Conference, Southern California, February

Women in the World Summit, New York City, April

Thrive (Huffington Post), New York City, April

California Women's Conference, Long Beach, CA, May

Forbes Women's Summit, New York City, May

TEDWomen, Sonoma, CA, May

S.H.E. Summit, New York City, June

Women Leading the Future, Washington, D.C., June

Omega Women & Power Conference, Rhinebeck, NY, September

Emerging Women, New York City, October

Pennsylvania Conference for Women, Philadelphia, October

Massachusetts Conference for Women, Boston, December

TEDxWomen (these happen all over the world simultaneously over a set time period)

Getting Started

If you are a first-time speaker or want to try out your talk in a more relaxed, intimate setting, here are some suggested venues that might be good for you. These only apply, of course, if the group has access to your target audience.

- workplace "lunch and learn" programs
- your alumni association
- your local library
- your local high school
- a community college
- a boutique bookstore
- your local YWCA chapter
- a local Meetup group

***

While you may never feel perfectly "ready" to give your talk, I want to encourage you to give your talk anyway. Your voice, your ideas and your soul on stage are what is needed to continue the awakening of feminine consciousness and bring our world into a healthier place for all.

Please don't keep silent what's inside of you any longer. Consider the words of Maya Angelou: "There is no greater agony than bearing an untold story inside of you."

I encourage you to step on stage and go for it!

Try this:

FEMININE LEADERSHIP PRACTICE

Step into your sacred space and set your timer for 5 minutes.

Owning the Stage. Since so many of us women have been socialized to not take up too much space, we have inhibited our physical expression and, accordingly, dampened our overall energetic presence. This does not bode well for being a powerful public speaker, since as women, much of our power and wisdom resides in our body. Today's leadership practice is designed to break this "glass ceiling."

- Stand comfortably in your sacred space with your feet hips-distance apart.
- Soften your eyes.
- Inhale and exhale through your nose a few times.
- Transition to walking your feet into a wider stance. Feet solidly on the floor.
- Breathe in and breathe out.
- Make fists with your hands, bring your hands up to your chest, and pound your chest with fervor, like a gorilla does when it wants to show its strength. While this behavior is typical for the male gorilla, and not the female, I want you to claim your female version of this. Give yourself permission to pound your chest and move your body in a way that asserts your strength.
- Add any sound that wants to come as you pound your chest.

- Next, transition to shaking out your arms, taking up as much space as you can. Shake your arms high. Shake your arms wide. Shake your arms low. Shake them as "loudly" as you can.
- Next, do this with your legs. Shake one leg high. Wide. Then low. Now do this with the other leg.
- Next, circle your hips, taking up as much space as you can. Moving in one direction, and then the other. Keep taking up space with your hips.
- Now invite in your belly and womb. Take up space with your belly and womb, as much space as you can. Circling, jiggling, whatever way your belly and womb want to move.
- Now walk your whole body through the space of the room. Take up as much space as you can. Hold your head up high. Spread open your shoulders and chest. Allow your arms to move. Your hips to move. Your belly to expand. Take up as much space as you can. Allow your energy to fill the space of the entire room. Keep walking and expanding. Breathe.
- After a minute, come back to your starting spot, stand and breathe. Keep your eyes open. Imagine your energetic body filling the space of the entire room. Stay grounded and present in your legs and hips as you do this. See yourself energetically expanding to the four corners of the room.

- Close your eyes and, keeping this same expanded self present, see yourself standing on stage in a large auditorium. Look around and see all who have come to listen to you. See the people in the farthest corners of the room, and expand your energy body to reach them. Let me know that you "see" them. Breathe. Smile.
- Enjoy some moments on stage in your mind's eye, and move about the stage gesticulating and taking up space in the most liberated and liberating way. Own the space.
- After a few moments, come back to the center of the stage and into stillness, feet and legs grounded, maintaining your large energetic presence. Imagine the words or sentiment you would like to leave with your audience. Be in that moment. Breathe.
- Slowly bring your hands to your heart, and honor this full expression of you. Know that you have access to this woman whenever you want to call on her. She is you.
- Finish by sounding one OM to close the practice.

FIND YOUR VOICE INTERVIEW

Take out your journal and a pen. Set a timer for 1 minute for each question. Answer each question in a stream-of-consciousness way. Do not edit yourself. Keep your pen to paper the whole time. Give yourself permission to truly express yourself.

1. What, if any, resistances are coming up for you as you work on (or think about working on) your signature talk?

2. What questions are coming up for you as you work on (or think about working on) your talk?

3. What is the biggest vision you have for yourself as a public speaker?

CHAPTER 12
Trailblazing Your Path to Change

"We will keep walking until peace, justice, and the rights of women is not a dream, but is a thing of the present."

– Leymah Gbowee

You wouldn't think of starting out on a hike you've never done before without clothing and shoes, food and water, a sleeping bag and tent, and without a map, right?

We've traveled together a long way in this book, and now we are about to say our goodbyes. Before we do that though, I want to make sure you properly equip yourself for your trailblazing journey.

This book was intended to serve as your map to show you where you are going, and provide you with the guidance you needed to get going on your trip. Now I'd like to talk to you for a moment about the food and water – the sustenance and support you're going to need – so you can make it all the way.

While the change you desire to create in the world may be right around the corner, it also may be very far off. It's important to be realistic about this. For instance, it took the suffragists nearly one hundred years, and a lot of hard work, to win women the right to vote in the United States through the passage of the 19th Amendment.

So how can you sustain yourself through what may be a

long, but very rewarding, journey?

Think about your support systems. Do you count on a supportive spouse or partner? A parent, sibling or other family member? A circle of friends or sisterhood? A mentor, teacher or coach? A therapist? An animal companion? All of these? Who can you call on for support when things get a bit grueling?

Also, think about what feeds you and nourishes you on a daily basis. Is it your yoga practice? Your daily run? Meditation? Music? A walk in the park? Healthy eating? Reading before bedtime? A good night's sleep?

For instance, I start my day with a yoga and meditation practice before my son gets up. On some mornings, when my husband is making breakfast for my son, I also go for a run. This helps me clear my mind and fills me with lots of positive energy for the day.

Then it's snuggle time and story time with my son. This is such a precious part of my day.

During the day, whenever I am working from home, I take "kitty breaks" to play with my cat, Max Frederick, and cuddle with him whenever he comes and visits me.

In the afternoon, I often go for a walk to take a break from the computer and enjoy a little nature time – sometimes by myself, sometimes with my son, and sometimes with a friend.

In the early evening, I enjoy playtime with my son, which often involves us making music, singing and dancing together. More reading time too.

At night, I talk and cuddle in with my husband, and, at least twice a month, gather in circle with my girlfriends or attend a women's event.

When it's time for bed, I pull out one of the books on my night table from where I draw inspiration. I read Gloria Steinem. I read Eve Ensler. I read Jean Shinoba Bolen. I read Brené Brown. I have a huge stack of books from feminist authors, and I am always discovering new ones.

I need all of this. I need to do my morning yoga. I need to have my playtime and cuddle time with my son, my husband and my kitty. I need quality time with my women friends. I need to attend women's circles and other women-only events. I need to sing, dance and make music. All of these things nourish me. This is what makes it possible for me to keep walking forward every day on my path.

What nourishes you? What do you need to feel supported?

Take a moment right now. Take a breath and reflect on these questions.

***

I believe that while we need to speak up, go out and be public with our activism, we also need time to be quiet, reflect and nurture our inner lives. As a feminine leader, you must remember that inner life is valuable.

As you continue your journey into greater leadership and trailblazing change, it's absolutely necessary for you to take time to rest, contemplate, and nourish yourself. This is essential to your feminine leadership.

While we used to think that we needed to emulate men to rise into leadership positions, and needed to deny our feminine nature in order to make it in a "man's world," today the story is different. The path to power is changing. I hope this book has helped you to see that.

Your leadership is about expanding into your feminine Truth, nourishing yourself from the inside out, circling up with those who support you, and bit by bit growing your circle of influence as you add more people – women and men, girls and boys – into the conversation and down the path of your vision.

Instead of an upward climb into leadership and influence, you have an opportunity to create a distinctly new model, one that is based on power *with*, rather than power over. Our leadership as women, once dependent on getting approval or permission from a patriarchal gatekeeper, no longer is about this. In the words of Maria Shriver: "You are the leader you've been looking for."

Envisioning Your Path to Change

So what does trailblazing your path to change look like for you?

Do you want to change laws? Do you want to change institutions? Do you want to change attitudes? Do you want to create new structures? Do you want to be a cultural activist, using your artistic expression to drive social and political change?

Trailblazing your path to change can come in many forms. It can come through writing, speaking, and artistry (as we have worked on in this book). It can come through teaching, mentoring, and becoming a philanthropist. It can come from building a business with a social mission, developing a social change project, and leading a social change movement. It can come from stepping into leadership positions in your community, in your workplace, and in your government.

It can come from a combination of these things, or something completely new that hasn't ever been done before, because it is unique to you and your blueprint.

Take a moment now to consider this question:

How are you inspired to use your leadership in the world?

While our roles and passions can shift over time (so never count anything out), I think it's important to look at what excites you right now, and where you feel you are most effective. I call these your "power spots."

What are your power spots? Take a moment and review the list below. Then write down your top three power spots. Be honest with yourself, and don't sell yourself short.

- Writing
- Speaking
- Artistry
- Teaching
- Mentoring
- Coaching
- Philanthropy
- Entrepreneurship
- Social Change Project Innovation
- Leading a Social Change Movement
- Leadership in Your Local Community
- Leadership in Your Workplace
- Business Leadership
- Political Leadership
- Religious/Spiritual Leadership
- Academia/Education Leadership
- Other: _____

After you have written down your list, consider how these three power spots connect and how you can hook these all up to be the engine that drives your ability to affect change.

How will you be trailblazing your path to change?

As we come to the end of this book, I want to acknowledge that trailblazing your path to change takes courage. It takes courage to have confidence in what you have to contribute. It takes courage to stretch yourself into new areas where you may feel uncomfortable, scared, or even terrified. It takes courage to stand in your truth, speak out and commit to the journey.

I believe you have this courage.

As Anne-Marie Slaughter wrote in her controversial article in *The Atlantic* in 2012, 'Why Women Still Can't Have it All': "Only when women wield power in sufficient numbers will we create a society that genuinely works for all women. That will be a society that works for everyone."

Your voice and your leadership matter. You are a vital part of a growing movement of women who are answering the call for feminine leadership. You no longer have to apologize for having an opinion, having a belief, or having a vision of how things should be. It is your right to express yourself. And furthermore, we are waiting for you.

Try this:

FEMININE LEADERSHIP PRACTICE

Step into your sacred space and set your timer for 5 minutes. This is the final leadership practice in the book. It's the one I want to leave you with to help you sustain and complete this journey. It's about connecting with what nurtures you. Enjoy!

Body Massage. Self-care and self-nurture are so important as you step out in a bigger way in the world. Knowing that you can nourish yourself through your own means is totally empowering, as well as a stress-reducer as you take on more responsibility and leadership. Take 5 minutes for this empowerment practice.

- Sit comfortably in your sacred space in your meditation position.
- Soften your eyes.
- Inhale and exhale through your nose a few times.
- Take your hands up to your head, and begin to gently massage around your temple, then your eyes, then your forehead, then your cheeks, your jaw, and then your entire scalp.
- Move your hands slowly down to your neck. Gently massage the back, sides and front of your neck.
- Then move to your shoulders. And then gradually down your arms to your hands and fingers.

- Continue the massage to your chest, your ribcage, your lower back, your hips, your buttocks, and then right on down your legs to your feet and toes.
- Allow your touch to be sensual, kind and nourishing.
- You can finish off with a "body wash" where you swoosh off any energetic remnants that are holding you down.
- Allow yourself to soak in the refreshing feeling of a self body-massage.
- Finish by sitting quietly for 1 minute, simply breathing.

FIND YOUR VOICE INTERVIEW

Take out your journal and a pen. Set a timer for 1 minute for each question. Answer each question in a stream-of-consciousness way. Do not edit yourself. Keep your pen to paper the whole time.

1. What have you discovered about yourself as a feminine trailblazer?

2. Who are the people in your life who you can reach out to for support and build community with as you step out into greater trailblazing leadership?

3. What is your greatest vision for your trailblazing leadership?

GO FORTH

Last year at the United Nations, UN Women Goodwill Ambassador and British actress, Emma Watson, launched the UN Women organization's HeForShe campaign, urging men and boys to advocate for gender equality. This is the first campaign of its kind at the United Nations.

When asked to take on this role, Emma shared that she had a lot of self-doubt and insecurity show up. She thought people might ask, *Who is this Harry Potter girl? And what is she doing up on stage at the UN?*

She confessed not knowing if she was qualified to be there, but what she did know for sure was that she cared about the problem, and wanted to make it better.

"In my nervousness for this speech and in my moments of doubt I've told myself firmly—if not me, who, if not now, when," said Emma.

As women, we tell ourselves so many stories about how we are not qualified enough, how we don't know enough of the "facts" or how we aren't cut out for politics or political conversation. While facts are important, I hope you've learned from this book that having a political voice goes much deeper than that.

It's about using your voice in a way that is aligned with your soul at the deepest level. I invite you to stick with this and keep it simple.

I hope you walk away from this book feeling more clear and confident about what you stand for; feeling absolutely clear that your voice matters; and feeling courageous and excited about using your voice and setting your leadership in motion.

When you do this, you will transform your life, and the lives of so many others along with you. You will make your contribution to healing the world.

I have come to believe that it's truly up to us as women to change things. We can't wait for permission any longer. We need to give it to ourselves.

If you have doubts and insecurities show up when opportunities are presented to you to step into your leadership, I hope Emma Watson's words might be helpful: *If not me, who? If not now, when?*

I leave you with my deepest wish – that you remember who you are from the deepest level of your soul, and that you trust this, and go forth with confidence and courage as a trailblazing feminine leader.

I am cheering you on. We all are cheering you on.

Come off of the sidelines. It's *your time*.

Tabby
April 2015

Acknowledgements

I want to acknowledge that writing this book was a big deal for me, as I have struggled often with my own voice. It is with deep gratitude that I want to honor my husband who walked with me every step of the way. Not only did he inspire me to write the book (I watched him write his own book just months prior), he encouraged me to take the leap, supported me in so many ways as I wrote, and served as my editor. The whole experience provided me with a deepened understanding and trust in feminine-masculine partnership. I am deeply grateful for this.

I'd like to thank my mom for being my mom and courageously raising me to pursue my own path. Although she felt that for much of her life she did not have a voice, she provided me with the love, trust and freedom to pursue my own. I also want to thank her for allowing me to interview her for this book.

I could not be where I am today without the loving sisterhood and encouragement of my good friends, Lotta Alsén, Bonnie Samotin, Reena Desai, Joanne Cohen, Cecily Miller, Christina Dunbar, Wendi Knox and Lisa Black. Each one of you has encouraged me and inspired me through your unique paths and the depth of who you are as women. I am deeply grateful for your sisterhood and for always seeing me and loving me as I am.

Thank you to all of my clients, who courageously show up week after week to dive into the depths of who you are, so you can reveal your truth and trailblaze your path to change. I am so moved by each one of you and the beautiful leadership that has emerged into the world because you have committed to your path. Special thanks to Connie Vasquez, Paige Nolan, and Rachel Keener who gave me permission to share their stories in this book. Thank you also to Paige for enthusiastically volunteering to be a reader for this book and supporting me through the final steps.

Thank you to my dear friend and former National Geographic colleague, Lili Weigart, for jumping in and saying yes to being a reader for the book. Lili's sharp mind, editorial prowess and big heart were invaluable as I inched my way closer to the finish line.

Thank you to Brett Donjon, another brilliant man on the team, who served as my copy editor. I appreciated Brett's clarity, warmth, expertise and dependability as we worked together.

Thank you to Michelle White Hart, who helped me see that I have a distinct methodology to my work and who coached me just prior to writing this book, supporting and encouraging me as I "vamped up" my visibility. These were significant steps to making it to the finish line.

Thank you to Maura Moynihan, whose loving soul and angelic presence nurtured me as I traversed some dark territory on my journey into greater leadership and visibility.

Thank you to my team of sister angels who lovingly jumped in to support me in getting the word out about the book. Elisa Parker, Judith Martinez, Sarah Moshman, Meggan Watterson, Amanda Young, Jen Duchene, Giselle Shapiro, Mary Collier, Yolanda Taylor Brignoni, Danika Gopcevic-Levesque, Rocio Ortega, Amie Williams, Jo Macdonald, Michele Christensen, Trista Hendren, Katharine Merriman, Alicia Heyburn, Joanna Lindenbaum, Katy DeBra, Elle Sompres, Rachel McCoskey Bennett, Dakota Smith, Karinna Hantula, Erin Leyba, Karin Robbins, Marcy Cole – thank you sisters. Your support means a lot to me.

I have deep gratitude for the pioneering women who

have come before me, who have mentored me in ways they may not know, and whose paths have inspired my leadership. Some of their voices are featured in this book, including Gloria Steinem, Maria Shriver, Eve Ensler, Marianne Williamson, Hillary Clinton and Katie Orenstein.

I want to thank my dad for being a great supporter of my blog and cheering me on as I blaze my trail. I am also grateful to my brothers, my sisters-in-law, and my nephews for always being so open, loving, and welcoming to "Aunt Tabby."

I am deeply grateful to my son, Bodhi, who challenges and inspires me on a daily basis. He, along with my cat, Max Frederick, bring so much joy to my every day. These two fellows are just a year apart in age, and, while little, are huge lights in my life. It is together with them and my husband that I walk this path of feminine leadership and being the leader that I was born to be.

And a huge bow of gratitude to you, dear reader, for showing up to read this book and courageously walking your path, joining a growing sisterhood of brave feminine trailblazers. We are rising together and supporting one another. Can you feel the power in that? Thank you for saying "yes" to your voice and to your leadership.

Resources

The following is a list of recommended resources for you to consider as you map out your steps for trailblazing change. I have chosen these groups because I have either partnered with them, written about them, or financially supported them at some point on my path. I personally endorse each one of them. I hope you will find a sisterhood of like-minded women somewhere on this list. Remember, we cannot do this alone. Changing the world takes a sisterhood.

Empowering Girls

Global Girl Media
www.globalgirlmedia.org

Girl Up
www.girlup.org

I Am That Girl
www.iamthatgirl.com

InHerShoes
www.inhershoesmvmt.com

Step Up
www.suwn.org

The Empowerment Project
www.empowermentproject.com

WriteGirl
ritegirl.org

Ending Violence Against Women

One Billion Rising
www.onebillionrising.org

UNiTE
endviolence.un.org

Promoting Women's Rights & Gender Equality

UN Women
www.unwomen.org

American Association of University Women
www.aauw.org

Half the Sky Movement
www.halftheskymovement.org

Feminist.com
www.feminist.com

Maternal Care

Every Mother Counts
www.everymothercounts.org

Amplifying Women's Voices in Media

Women's Media Center
www.womensmediacenter.com

The OpEd Project
www.theopedproject.org

International Women's Media Foundation
www.iwmf.org

MAKERS
www.makers.com

See Jane Do
www.seejanedo.com

Supporting Women in Politics

Women's Campaign Fund
www.wcfonline.org

National Women's Political Caucus
www.nwpc.org

EMILY's List
www.emilyslist.org

She Should Run
www.sheshouldrun.org

Microloans for Women

Catapult
www.catapult.org

Kiva
www.kiva.org

Philanthropy

Malala Fund
www.malalafund.org

Women for Women International
www.womenforwomen.org

Women in the World Foundation
www.thedailybeast.com/witw.html

Women Moving Millions
www.womenmovingmillions.net

Women's Circles & Feminine Spirituality

The Los Angeles Goddess Collective
www.meetup.com/goddesscollectivela

The Millionth Circle
www.millionthcircle.org

Reveal
www.megganwatterson.com/reveal-the-event

Environmental Action & Sustainability

Women's Earth & Climate Action Network
www.wecaninternational.org

Mothers Out Front
www.mothersoutfront.org

Animal Rights Advocacy

Humane Society of the United States
www.hsus.org

What's Next?

I hope that this book has inspired you and provided you with the tools you need to claim your voice, take a stand in your leadership and start creating the change you desire to see in the world.

If you want to go further and do more, I encourage you to visit my website to learn about my group classes and private coaching programs. You can find me at tabbybiddle.com.

ABOUT THE AUTHOR

Tabby Biddle is a women's rights advocate, writer and leadership coach, specializing in helping women find their voice. Her work has been featured by prominent national and international media including, *The Huffington Post*, the *Los Angeles Times*, *USA Today, UN Dispatch*, Current TV and National Public Radio.

A United Nations Foundation press fellow, Tabby has met with world leaders, political dignitaries, high-level policymakers and global decision-makers to help expand the dialogue around women's rights and global issues affecting women and girls.

She is the Director of the Los Angeles Goddess Collective, a community of women leaders and emerging leaders at the intersection of feminine spirituality, creative expression and social change.

Through her speaking appearances, group classes and private coaching practice, Tabby has supported hundreds of women on their path into leadership – from business leaders, to media personalities, to celebrity activists, to artists, to students, to entrepreneurs.

Tabby received her Masters in Education from Bank Street College in New York City and her undergraduate degree in Political Science from Colby College. She lives in Santa Monica, CA, with her husband, toddler son and cat. Learn more at tabbybiddle.com.

Follow Tabby on Twitter: @tabbybiddle

Follow Tabby on Facebook: Tabby Biddle (Author)

Made in the USA
Middletown, DE
15 January 2018